The Galilee Story

The Story of a Small Gospel Record Label
with a Good Idea

Ivan Caldwell, Malachi Doyle, Neale Farnell, Sally Hilder,
Anne Levitch, Genna Levitch, Lester Silver, Lowell Tarling,
Stewart Walker, Robert Wolfgramm

© Copyright 2014;
Ivan Caldwell, Malachi Doyle, Neale Farnell, Sally Hilder,
Anne Levitch, Genna Levitch, Lester Silver, Lowell Tarling,
Stewart Walker and Robert Wolfgramm

All rights reserved. Without limiting the rights under copyright reserved above, no part of this work/publication may be reproduced, stored in or introduced into a retrieval system, or transmitted, in any form or by any means (electronic, mechanical, print, photocopying, recording or otherwise), without the prior written permission of the copyright owners.

Music/general

A copy of this book can be found in the National Library of Australia

Cover design: Joel Tarling
Cover photograph: Carl Needham
Other images & photographs: individual authors
Editor: Lowell Tarling lowell@lowelltarling.com.au
www.lowelltarling.com.au

Book creation: *Linda Ruth Brooks Publishing*

ISBN: 978-0-6484077-3-7

Sponsored by

galilee

www.galileerecords.com.au
for CD's, lyrics, archives and more

The authors have taken all possible care to give appropriate acknowledgement and seek permission from all interested parties and welcome any further correspondence. Enquiries should be addressed to the publisher.

Persecution Games, Lowell, Genna & Robert, *All My Friends Are Sinners*, Apocalypse Rider, Apocalypse Rider performance; Avondale College Chapel 1999

Table Of Contents

Jesus People - Genna Levitch & Lowell Tarling 1
Galilee - A Sociological Recollection - Robert Wolfgramm 5

1 - Dave Caldwell - Ivan Caldwell 7
2 - Jimmy Little, The Wayfarers & Louis Rao's Band - Lowell Tarling 17
3 - It Was 1964 - Stewart Walker 28
4 - Brass Bands, Other Bands - Robert Wolfgramm 36
5 - Uncle Bill Wolfgramm - Lowell Tarling 44
6 - The Road To Mackay And Back - Robert Wolfgramm 48
7 - Threedom Years - Lowell Tarling 56
8 - Salt, Thomas & Jonah - Lester Silver 68
9 - Jonah, Pact Folk, Sally - Lowell Tarling 76
10 - Melbourne Streetpreachers - Robert Wolfgramm 84
11 - Playing On Galilee - Genna Levitch 92
12 - Who Is Sally Hilder? - Sally Hilder 98
13 - An Interview With Robert Wolfgramm - 1980 115
14 - Persecution Games Recording Sessions 1978-83 Robert Wolfgramm 128
15 - Persecution Revolution, 1980-1982 - Lowell Tarling 134
16 - Damn Right, I Got The Blues -Neale Farnell 146
17 - Apocalypse Riders, 1998 - Malachi Doyle 152
18 - Support Act - Anne Levitch 160
19 - Of Music, Mice & Men - Dr Robert Wolfgramm 164
Appendix 185
Seven Waves Of Australian Rock - Robert Wolfgramm 186
Author Credits 192
Glossary 194
Review & Media Release 198

Who drove crosscountry seventytwo hours to find out if I had a vision or you had a vision or he had a vision to find out Eternity

Allen Ginsberg, *Howl*

Jesus People

Genna Levitch & Lowell Tarling

In between performing his hit songs on stage, Elvis Presley would sing hymns. We can only guess that, as he was brought up singing in a church choir, he couldn't shake the habit. It now sounds a bit weird though. Where is there any crossover from the soaring humbleness of *Amazing Grace* to the self-obsessed fashion victim of 'don't step on my blue suede shoes?'

Maybe it went a lot deeper, as all the original Rockers were from the deeply religious American south. Most were black. Rock and Roll drew from its southern, black religious influences. Even if the music was 'of the Devil', it was sung with religious fever and amazing power.

One of the original hysterical, screaming madmen was Little Richard. A devoted Seventh-day Adventist who believed it was *all* gospel. In concerts he would drop on one knee and howl that 'this is healing music, it makes the blind to see, the lame to walk, the dead to raise up!' Then one day he took off his flashy rings and threw a King's fortune of jewels into the sea, he turned away from Rock and Roll and went back to playing piano in his SDA Church in New York.

Rock and Roll had too much religion in it. The churches knew that and they also knew that they were being plagiarised. They fought tooth and nail to exterminate it, as there was no way they could match it. Another generation of youth was about to be lost to the unholy trinity of sex, drugs and rock and roll.

Except... except... there were a few, a small number... a remnant... who believed they could take the Devil's music and bring it back to where it belonged. To take the power of Rock and meld it with the power of the gospel! It was a dangerous undertaking; like taming rattlesnakes, playing with dynamite, entering the enemy's camp. It would take talent, blind faith and supreme self-confidence. It could only be done by being better musically and lyrically than popular songs. It could only be done speaking the language of today with the clarity, passion and truth of the original gospel of hope.

In June 1971, Jesus made the cover of *Time* magazine. In October of the same year, he did it again, this time as *Jesus Christ Superstar*. Internationally-speaking, we might therefore date the Jesus wing of the Hippie movement to 1971, although there had certainly been Hippies-for-Jesus in California since about 1968.

Christian parents probably would never accept religion as one of centre-pieces of Hippie counter-culture. That's because Christian parents didn't accept that Buddhism, Tarot cards, astrology, the *Tibetan Book of the Dead* and all that New Age stuff was religion at all. Anti-religion, if anything. But it was indeed 'religion' though not one universally attractive to all Hippies.

The Christian Hippies staged their counter-coup and emerged in the early-70s bringing with them, guitars, drums and hair. The older generation was hugely threatened and denounced all this as 'worldly' whereas, these things were never the heart of the matter. In fact theologically, Christian Hippies were fundamentalists, often with the same kind of apocalyptic fervour and emphasis on the Book of Revelation, usually associated with 'fringe' religions and cults.

Religion was of course not new to Pop Culture. Rock n Roll music, so despised by the churches and the parents, was itself a hybrid of many musical styles, one of them being 'Gospel'.

Weirdly, many of the early Rockers, like Elvis Presley and Little Richard, recorded albums of 'favourite hymns' as an aside to their mainstream chart success. But by the late-60s Rock musicians were putting their religion centre-stage. Beatle, George Harrison did it with *My Sweet Lord*, in praise of his Lord Krishna, and English super-group Blind Faith recorded *In the Presence of the Lord* which young Christians at the time picked as a reference to 1 Samuel 6:20 ('Who can stand in the presence of the Lord, this Holy God?'). But these people were Pop stars, not 'Jesus People'.

The first full-blown Christian LP record by a Jesus-Person-Hippie-Christian was singer Larry Nelson's *Upon This Rock* (1969). Released by Capital Records, it was a commercial flop. But his 1971 release, *Only Visiting this Planet*, was noticed by young Christians everywhere. The record re-defined what Christians could do with music and gave legitimacy to guitars and drums, so strongly associated as the Devil's instruments throughout the 1960s.

Most 60s teenage Christians spent that decade arguing with their parents about music. Preachers denounced the Beatles, asked converts to destroy Rock records and fulminated against guitars (and especially against drums). And most teenagers disagreed. They put their religion in one compartment and their culture in another. That was the 1960s for most teens who wanted to remain Christian.

In 1971, everything changed, not least that the first wave of young ministers were taking their place in the pulpits, noting that their parents' generation was alienating their youth. Acoustic guitars started replacing organs as the instrument of worship. For starters, guitars were portable, handy for street-witnessing, good for singing in parks and ideal in Christian coffee shop environments.

All Protestant churches went through these changes and the Seventh-day Adventists were probably level-pegging with the rest. While the older ministers railed against Rock music, not being musicians themselves, they said dopey things. They got laughed at behind their backs and young people often took to worshipping separately from the oldies.

The Anglicans were doing it. The newly-formed Uniting Church was doing it. They were all about the same, and in these matters the Seventh-day Adventists were neither ahead nor behind the other churches. What did set the Seventh-day Adventists somewhat apart from the rest however, was that they added to this cultural 'war' a theological dispute.

Rather than using the word 'Gospel' as a general term for religious stuff, to Adventist young people of the 70s it meant Cross-centred theology. Not only were many young people prepared to argue with their parents about guitars and drums, but also about the very heart of the Christian faith. This startled some Protestant circles, who had long ago written the Adventists off as a cult. Now, they wanted to know what was going on inside this once 'legalistic' church!

The connection between Adventism and guitars in Australia probably goes way back to the earliest forms of Australian Country music. It was rumoured that Slim Dusty's mate, Shorty Ranger was a Seventh-day Adventist, and maybe he played his instrument in the Kempsey Church. Likewise, New Zealander, Ted Bennett was a known guitarist, and again – if he played guitar in church in the early 60s or before, we didn't know. What the Sydney Adventists knew about guitars was there was something happening in the Hurstville Church, Guildford Church, and then in the mid-60s out of the Thornleigh Church came a guitar/drums unit that looked very much like people who'd appeared on Bandstand. Mod clothes, long hair and poise. However, they didn't perform in church. That sort of thing didn't happen until the 70s.

Galilee - A Sociological Recollection

Robert Wolfgramm

There we were in the dining room of the Robbie and Lowell's West Ryde home in September 1977. A white feller with black ancestors (Lowell), a black feller with white ancestors (me), and a Jew named originally after the Aussie bush poet, Lawson - all excited about the prospects for the first vinyl artist to feature on our Biblically named label (Galilee): a part-Maori teenage girl named Sally Hilder. French-Malagasy-English, Tongan-Fijian-German, Russian-Sephardic-Jew, and New Zealand-Maori – welcome to late 70s Australian multiculturalism. And all of us half-in and half-out of Australian Adventism, itself an adaptation of a mid 19th Century Methodist American sub-cult.

From Melbourne and Sydney, we were a teacher, a truck-driver, a dentist, and a student. What the heck were we doing there? How did we even get together? Find each other?

I have no conclusive idea in terms of specifics why each of us as individuals, but sociologically we were as predictable as Melbourne rain in winter. In contrast to the Anglo-conformist stereotype of the first half of the 20th Century, Australia post-Gough Whitlam (1972-75) was now made up of millions like us. Not even isolationist Adventism could hold out the interpenetration of ethnic minorities into its heartlands on the North Shore, Wahroonga, in the inner urban west, Strathfield, and further north-west, Cooranbong.

There we, or rather types like us, were bound to mix and match at some point: the demographic stats of the post-White Australia policy were in favour of it. Al Grassby had championed it through the wooden attitudes of union Labor, and Malcolm Fraser guaranteed it over the heads of his rabid-right Country Party colleagues.

Thanks Al, thanks Mal. Without you *Galilee* would never have been.

A few months later, the multicultural and post-60s potpourri got even more interesting when the three of us (Genna, Lowell and I) met three Anglo-Australians who would play a critical role in our first vinyl release,

First was a similarly displaced North Shore Anglo-Adventist Australian, Paul Bryant, an engineer who headed up the Gosford-located Jam Studios. Paul, in turn, led us to a second- generation Kiwi-Aussie guitarist, Mick Reid, who, just around the corner from his Blue Mountains home, showed us the door to Charlie Hull - arranger, keyboard player and bandleader. These encounters and eventual collaborations were serendipitous chances perhaps, but in our case, given the parameters we set for our project – ie. to be the best Christian music of the time - it was unavoidable that the 'new kids on the block' (us) should meet the 'old heads' (them); the inexperienced Galilee trio merging with experienced, Jam Studio musos.

The thing is, what looks like a predetermined plan in life is never experienced as such. No, this was exciting. Predestination can only be dull robotic acting out of rote-acquired roles. This wasn't that. This was not knowing a thing, not knowing who was what, who was where, who was why. Sorting it all out and getting the outcomes we did was hilarious, dramatic fun - the most fun of my life.

Yes, we gave ourselves roles – Genna you be the manager, Lowell you be the song editor, and me, I'll be the music producer - but we all strayed into each other's yards, as friends will when something new is at stake, when it's a first-time experience.

But it obviously worked – the proof is in the pudding. That is, we are still close friends and our output together lives on and has value to many, three and a half decades later. Hence, the rereleased albums on Psalter, the website, and this book.

1

Dave Caldwell

Ivan Caldwell

My father obviously has had a great influence on my life and Bob and Lowell's as well.

'Uncle Dave'

Dave Caldwell was a music man and he loved to share his music.

Many, especially in Adventist circles, knew him as the Cello Fellow. The cello was his main instrument and he really could make it sing. I remember the emotion just pouring out of that instrument the day he played at his sister's funeral. Dave was lead cellist for many years in the Ku-ring-gai Chamber Orchestra. Over the years he also played piano, violin and cello in several trios. As a schoolteacher he had always enjoyed producing school concerts - they were his forte.

The *Renardi Trio* was the best known of these groups. Dave found a soulmate in Glenn Nixon, the violinist, and their music was in great demand. I remember sitting through many hours of performances in churches all around Sydney. As a whole family we went to places I had never heard of, having to confront a Sabbath School and a church full of new faces each week. My siblings, Ronnie, Brian, Jolie and I found it quite intimidating but we sure met a lot of people.

We went to Lithgow several times where a grand Saturday night concert would also be part of the occasion, as well as the morning and afternoon services. We would all stay overnight, billeted out amongst various church families. This was also quite daunting, with my brother and sisters being split up to stay with different families. Sometimes it worked out well - my younger brother Brian became quite infatuated with one girl that he met in our travels.

At those concerts, Dad would release his larrikin side. On those Saturday nights he would bring out the mouthorgan, guitar and melodica. This latter, he used in a skit where he would eventually play the melodica with a vacuum cleaner on blow cycle! This saved much huffing, puffing and running out of breath.

Dad loved collecting musical instruments. Like the banjo he bought for one pound at a Wahroonga School Fete. And the double bass that had been damaged in a car accident, that he bought cheaply and repaired so it sounded as good as new. Add to these a steel-stringed acoustic guitar, piano-accordion, chromatic mouthorgan, chord mouthorgan plus various odd instruments like ocarina and nose flute. All of these he could play.

Dad was also quite accomplished on the piano. I was very impressed one day when he sat down and started playing Beethoven's *Moonlight Sonata* from memory. He could not play it right through but it showed that he'd had some good piano lessons as a child.

For a while Dad was leader of the *Northern Fellowship*, a youth group that met regularly on Friday nights and went away on camping trips. The song services were always joyous and full of gusto. Dad would encourage musicians like Vern Wilkinson - quite a talented trumpet player - to join in and lead out. He had John Truscott on piano and a talented musician named Graham Fletcher who played marimba, vibraphone and glockenspiel beautifully. Glenn Nixon would often be there on violin and other musicians who were willing to join in.

Dad also loved folk music. He made big song charts out of butcher's paper on which he would write out folk songs from all around the world. These were used at school and at the occasional 'Hootenanny' at our home. Dad invited musos like Dave Hall, Kevin Were, Alvyn Backhouse with their wives, girlfriends and other singers to join in great sing-a-long and jam sessions. It was enormous fun.

It was a rich musical environment. My own journey into the world of music began in my younger years by just being a listener and observer. My first instrument was a ukulele given to me when I was about 11 years old. Now, over fifty years later, I still have it hanging on the wall, next to a few newer ones, in my music room. Along with 100 others, my wife Deb and I are members of the *Central Coast Ukulele Club*. It is one of the most enjoyable activities of my retirement, having just taken us to Hawaii to participate in a large Ukulele Festival over there. It's funny how things go full cycle.

Like all of my siblings, I had a go at learning piano. I only lasted about twelve months before giving up. The raps on the knuckles from a tough teacher and the strict practice regime were enough to discourage me. Of the four of us, my sister Jolie was the most successful at mastering this instrument. She now has Mum and Dad's piano in her home.

Before taking up the trumpet, my brother Brian had to suffer some lessons on the violin. It suited him much better and Dad had him playing in a brass band for a while. Brian has inherited many of Dad's instruments including the double bass and all his mouth organs. He has added to this collection with dozens of guitars and ukuleles hanging off his walls. And he plays them all too, posting songs every week in the *Ukulele Underground* worldwide competitions.

My Dad taught me cello for several years until I headed off to Wagga Wagga Teachers College. I reached a reasonable level of competence and even started playing in the Ku-ring-gai Chamber Orchestra with him. I also played in a couple of musical events at the Teachers College. But I never continued with the cello lessons and felt my playing was rather mediocre. So I let the cello playing slide away. Though he never said so, it must have disappointed my Dad. The beautiful cello I inherited from him now sits in the corner of my music room. Occasionally I dust it off and use it to play hymns at church.

Guitar playing and singing became my next passion. This was also because of Dad's influence. When we went camping at Norah Head each Christmas holidays those big song charts would come out and we would sit around playing and singing. Various instruments would be brought out and shared around. It was here that I first started learning chords on banjo and guitar. And I found I really enjoyed singing.

While standing in the pews at Wahroonga Church each Sabbath, to sing four or five verses of some long-winded hymn, it became a personal challenge to me to sing the harmonies. I would practice sight-reading the soprano, alto, tenor then the bass. Looking back, I really appreciate the way the hymn books were written in four-part harmony.

I sang in a boys' choir at Wahroonga Church for a few months, conducted by Mr French. While at Wagga Wagga Teachers College I was surprised to find myself given a lead role, as King Gama, in Gilbert and Sullivan's *Princess Ida*. Dad and Mum were startled to receive a newspaper clipping in the mail of their son in full costume and make-up and hardly recognisable. (There were two King Gamasin the photo because I had only taken on the role with the proviso that I be excused from performing on my Sabbath.)

It was while at Wagga that I remember doing my first solo at church using a guitar as accompaniment. I distinctly recall being so nervous that my knees were shaking. The man responsible for encouraging me to perform was Ross Corny, a friend from those Lithgow concerts with

Dad. He also had me singing duets with Robina Bastion who was teaching at the Wagga Adventist School at that time. As I have sung in many churches since then, Ross Corny would often remind me about his role in starting my singing career.

I was only eighteen when I graduated from Teachers College. This was because I was in the last year of the old 5-year Leaving Certificate at High School. Students in the class behind me, like Lowell Tarling, Andrew Kingston, Greg Parr, Jenny Petherbridge and John Pye, had to go on and do a sixth year. The Teaching Certificate only took me two years so I was pushed through the system rather quickly.

In my first year of teaching at Fairfield West Public School I joined some other teachers to form a folk-singing quartet similar to the Seekers. I used the old double bass that Dad had repaired and we got brave enough to perform on Channel Ten's *New Faces*. We actually won that night and were given two performance 'gigs' as a prize. We sang in a restaurant at Randwick and at a pub in Manly Vale. This gave us enough incentive to name ourselves *The Archers*, dress ourselves in paisley shirts and chase up various gigs in clubs and restaurants around the Fairfield area. It was all great experience but my heart wasn't really in it.

I did continue to play double bass for a few more years. First, I teamed up with Andrew Kingston and the Van Dykes, a husband and wife singing duo, to form a gospel quartet. Then, I started playing bass for Warren Judd with *The Commission* after Carl Needham left them. Dad's old double bass got recorded onto vinyl when ART produced their first album, *Souled On Him*. I also got to sing my first recorded solo on that album with just the first line of the song, *Miracle Of Grace*. Later, I became a singer with *Commission* when Dave McMahon took over as bass player.

One of the biggest influences on me musically, however, was Robert Wolfgramm. Bob came to live with us for several years while going to school in Sydney.

I went off to Teachers College for two of those years so I wasn't around all the time. I remember him initially as a shy little Fijian boy who became a younger brother to me.

Dad, of course, got him involved in music and had him playing tuba in a brass band. I remember hearing about him lugging that instrument, which was as big as he was, around the streets of Sydney in the Anzac Day march.

His Mum found out that she could get more financial support from the government if she sent him to a boarding school, so Bob was sent to Lilydale Academy in Melbourne about the same time that I was finishing at Teachers College. He would still come and stay with us during the holiday breaks and it was then that he would share his music with me.

Bob's interest and skills in music really blossomed while he was at Lilydale and I was so lucky to be included in the musical journey.

Bob absorbed music of all genres and his talent as a guitar player far surpassed mine, so there was a lot he could teach me. It was fascinating to sit with him and go through the metrical index in the back of the hymnal, replacing the melody lines of traditional hymns. *What a Friend We Have In Jesus* and *Come Just As You Are* were two examples of songs with his tunes that I started singing around Sydney. They were also the first to be recorded on the ART album, *Let the Son Shine*.

It was while we were sitting on the veranda of our home in Strathfield one holiday playing *Come Just As You Are* that Dad came out and made a suggestion. He told Bob that he wrote such beautiful melodies he needed to start writing his own words to match. Bob still refers to this as a 'watershed' moment. He did start writing his own beautiful gospel songs with powerful messages.

Each song Bob wrote showed his musical growth, from a very simple folk style in *Troubles and Woe (Poor Man's Lament)* to the more jazz oriented *Crucifix*. I remember him being very proud of the three distinct sections of his first *Emmaus* song. I loved the way Bob would always have a Biblical text next to the title of each song he wrote, showing the origin of the thought behind its message. It was such a privilege to be a recipient of these beautiful gospel songs.

Having these original songs from a fresh source, other than Ralph Carmichael, Jimmy Owens and all the other American songwriters led to quite a few requests for them to be heard.

With Bryan Craig, Bruce Judd, John Banks, Russ Gibbs and Warren Judd encouraging lots of youth involvement during the SALT era, it was a great time to be involved in gospel music. I was the only one performing Bob's songs around Sydney at that time, so they were quite unknown and well received.

By the time the live *Salt In Concert* album was recorded there was a large group of young people involved in creating and performing gospel music.

Many of the songs at that concert were originals by singer/songwriters like Bruce Judd, Lester Silver, Bev and Chris Till, Genna Lawson and Lucille Lees, Brian Patterson and Robert Wolfgramm. Read the credits on the album cover and you will see the names of the many singers and instrumentalists who also made this a wonderful inspirational pooling of the talents of that time.

I performed Bob's song *Holy Spirit* at that concert, and he was there to hear it. Bob was at Avondale College by then and just happened to be down visiting me for the weekend. I tried to talk him into performing one of his songs with me but he declined.

What he did do however was write a second verse to *Holy Spirit* in the back of my car as we were driving over from my unit in Homebush to the Wahroonga Activity Centre for the concert. It was literally 'hot off the press'. And the backing players were fantastic. If you listen to the track you will hear some marvellous acoustic guitar playing as Dave Wilmoth, who had never seen or heard the song before, just started to warm up as the song finished.

While Bob was at Avondale College he collaborated with Lowell Tarling to write a musical about Jesus called *Threedom*.

It started out as a group of songs tied together with narration. It was first performed at Hamilton, Newcastle by a small band of musicians including Dad on cello. During several more performances it evolved with more songs and chorus interludes added. The instrumental backing grew into a mini orchestra. Bob spent many hours writing a full orchestral score.

Before it was allowed to be performed at Avondale College, it had to be approved and censored by some of the staff there. My Dad, who had many musical ties with the college, found himself defending this folk cantata in which he was playing. His support did not stop the axing of *Herod's Song*, which was to have been sung by my younger brother, Brian. It was narrated rather than sung.

The initial performance of the expanded version of *Threedom* was at Parramatta SDA Church, where it attracted a large audience who had come to hear this ambitious and somewhat controversial cantata. My father and I were proud to have been a part of this wonderful endeavour.

Lowell and Bob went on to co-write more gospel songs. Many were written specifically for street preaching. They were a powerful tool when song from the back of a truck in the streets of Newcastle or Melbourne. They were also performed in a much more Rock-oriented style in contrast with the soft folk renditions of their songs that I usually presented.

After they had built up quite a large repertoire of songs they teamed up with their friend Genna Levitch to start a record label, *Galilee*. They produced three albums. The first, *All My Friends Are Sinners*, featured a young schoolgirl, Sally Hilder, singing Lowell and Bob's songs.

Bob eventually overcame his shyness and reluctance to record his own material when they did the second album, initially titled, *Bob* (now *Refugee*). I remember attending some of the recording sessions and the final mix-downs with Bob and his sound engineer, Paul Bryant. Bob learned a lot from working with the studio musicians. I know he is still friends with the guitarist, Mick Reid.

Two young girls, the Wragg sisters Liane and Michele, were used as backing singers on some tracks. Both these ladies now attend the same church as me at Erina and they look back fondly on the experiences they had working with Bob on this album.

For the third album, *Persecution Games*, Bob did not use Charlie

Hull, who had been the arranger for the first two albums. Bob enlisted the help of friends to help with the recording. You will hear Lowell's voice as well as mine on some tracks. There is a male quartet singing *Jesus Keep Me Near the Cross*. A solo piano plays *Just As I Am*. Bob does quiet guitar versions of *Vinegar* and *Save Your Grace*. But, it also featured the much raunchier and raw sound of a heavy Rock band on tracks like *Persecution Games*.

With this album Galilee branched into a heavier Rock genre, which was not to everyone's taste. The startling cover featuring a Martin Sharp painting of a distorted Luna Park Face with a dingo in its jaws was also quite confronting.

I admire Bob, Lowell and Genna enormously for the brave way they ventured into the record-producing industry and what they achieved with the Galilee label.

I was to have more involvement with Lowell when I helped with the musical *Jonah*, which he co-wrote with Lester Silver. Dave Hall, Geoff Heise and myself were the band. Prior to this, Lester had also written his own musical called *Thomas*, which he, myself and Dave Hall played in. It was great to have church leaders like John Banks and David Weslake around at that time to support projects like these.

Gospel music has been a passion for me largely due to the influence of people like Bob and Lowell. I have never stopped playing their music. There is hardly ever a sermon preached when I can't say to myself, 'I know a Wolfgramm-Tarling song that would complement this message beautifully'.

My father obviously has had a great influence on my life and probably Bob and Lowell's as well.

I know Dad had a soft spot for Lowell back in high school when he was a challenging, talented and creative student. He recognised a kindred larrikin spirit right from the start. He loved Bob's enormous talent and followed his career closely down through the years.

There was never a time that my father said, 'No' to a request for cello accompaniment to songs that my wife and I, or my brother, Brian, were learning. He loved playing Bob's songs.

When he turned 80 and threatened to put the cello away for good Brian, Debbie and I sat down with him and recorded dozens of songs that he performed with us over the years.

His cello playing may be a little below the standard that he set in his prime but this CD recording, titled *Giving Thanks,* is now a precious family heirloom.

2
Jimmy Little, The Wayfarers & Louis Rao's Band

Lowell Tarling

The Wayfarers were the first SDA band I'd ever heard of, with drums, bass and electric guitars.

The Wayfarers: Allan Butler, Tony Roy and Trevor Roy

The first Australian Christian minister to harness Rock music that we were aware of was Rev Ted Noffs, who returned from his ministry in the Riverina NSW and became engaged in the neat, softly-spoken, short haired Brian Henderson's *Bandstand* - an inspiration to Noffs because Henderson was a 'square'. Noffs copied Henderson's approach when he opened his *Teenage Cabaret* in the Central Methodist Mission's Fellowship House. It attracted 600 young people every Saturday. Among them an Aboriginal boy from Redfern called Jimmy Little.

17

Jimmy came into the Methodist church in 1962 and, under Noffs' guidance, he recorded *Royal Telephone* which went to No 1 in the Australian charts. We all noticed that – a *Gospel* song on the Australian Pop charts. Jimmy Little played an acoustic-electric guitar, (not quite the evil instrument) and where he used drums, they were indiscernible. In fact, his hit song could be legitimately performed in church, in the Song Service, Special Item, Saturday Night Socials or any church venues.

Tony Roy and his drums

'Groups' per se, were nothing new to the church. The ideal type was the *a cappella* male quartet with an uplifting name, like *The King's Heralds*. The 'folk group' was another acceptable type. That is, a chick singer accompanied by two guys. Peter, Paul & Mary (without the beards) was the correct look.

These sorts of groups often sang Special Items in and around church services. Allan Broadhurst, Clayton Simms (my friends) and I would be forced to sit through *Kumbaya*, *I Believe* and whatever else they performed in church. So in the early 1960s we never, *ever,* saw a group with drums at any church-sponsored event. That wouldn't be a group, but a band. And in those days, all good church folk knew that bands were wicked.

One day, classmate Greg Parr told me such a wicked band had been formed at the Hurstville SDA Church. The personnel were Allan Butler, John Furness, Clive Sandon, Terry Grace and two brothers (whose cousin I would someday marry) Trevor and Tony Roy. Their name was *The Wayfarers*. They'd sat in on a couple of Bee Gees jam sessions, Greg told me this, but the only thing I heard was 'Tony Roy on drums'. Yes, drums.

Greg played pedal-steel guitar and I learned to strum chords. So Greg reckoned we could pull off instrumentals like *Apache* and *Bombora*. Okay. So we added Edu Neirinckx, who half-heartedly played harmonica, Colin Mead on drums – though he never did buy that kit. And Andrew Kingston & Tom Borody who, between them, played everything – clarinet, keyboards, bass and probably Edu's harmonica when he couldn't be bothered with it.

We called ourselves *The Rejects* and it was a class band.

The Rejects L-R Greg Parr, Lowell Tarling, Tom Borody, Edu Neirinckx, (Andrew Kingston absent)

Various combinations of the outfit backed other class members as required. Like singers Janette Hughes, Jenny Petherbridge and Adrian Jones at concerts and parties.

However, I never did like surf music. The Rolling Stones were waiting for me around the next bend. I jumped onto that wagon, pushing to play *Tell Me* instead of *Pipeline* at rehearsals. I quit *The Rejects*, which no one really noticed.

Instead, I carried my guitar back-and-forth from Allan's place to mine, and played there, usually when dodging church. Allan, Clayton and I probably should have formed something. Both he and Clayton bought guitars, but teaching them wasn't easy. Although Allan had no problem playing riffs, he had immense difficulty learning barre chords. Clayton was an entirely different proposition. He launched straight into learning tricky jazz chords, which meant he could never keep time, trying to cram all those passing chords between the obvious ones (which Allan and I favoured).

Meanwhile, we heard that a band had sprung out of the Thornleigh SDA Church. Fronted by Dave and Phillip Quick, two snappy dressers with Mod haircuts, they looked terrific. And that was good enough for us. That was the main bit! Also in the band was David Gow, a tall guy we nicknamed 'Entwistle' (ie. *The Who)* because he played bass. And Harry Dustin (later, Harry Young) on drums.

For the next three months I thought I was a pretty good guitar player, after which I never really improved. During this period, with Bob Dylan ringing in my head, I carried my guitar everywhere. I played it on public transport, on the school verandah and at lunchtime I often jammed with a younger guitarist, Louis Rao. These bashes drew a small audience, which is where I noticed Robert Wolfgramm who was three years younger than me. I recall lending him music stuff, maybe sheet music or LP records. Also in the audience, discreetly positioned up the back, Genna Levitch sometimes dropped by and quietly observed.

The real world of Rock seemed so distant, but it was much closer than we thought. Allan's brother Kevin (aka Brian Vogue) was somewhat older than us. A businessperson at heart, Kevin established the *Linda Lee* record label, releasing as his first single, *How Great Thou Art* by respected church singer, Jan Judd. His next single was *Poison Ivy* by Billy Thorpe & the Aztecs which famously kept the Beatles from the #1 spot on the Sydney charts at the very moment that they made their first and only tour of Australia.

This Broadhurst-brotherly connection did not bring us within the orbit of the Aztecs. The closest I got was finding guitarist Vince Melouney's plectrum in the back of Kevin's Jaguar car.

All this was shortly before and around 1965, the year I bashed the crap out of my guitar. I learned lots of songs, gained heaps of confidence and wrote a song called *Irene*. Written to the chords of *Keep On Running* (backwards), Allan and Clayton were impressed. Everyone was. Louis was impressed. Even my cousin Stewart Walker was impressed. Stewart was the first person I'd seen playing guitar at church functions. He was a regular performer at his Guildford SDA Church social evenings. Stewart sang Elvis songs like, *I Can't Help Falling In Love With You* and *Wooden Heart*. But his big number, the one all the old dears all loved, was his take on the Marty Robbins song, *El Paso*.

Stewart's parents bought me my first *Belmont* guitar, he taught me how to play chords. Gradually I played passably well enough to strum behind him on *He'll Have to Go*. And then Stewart changed.

Forsaking his fan club of 60-year old dears, Stewart unexpectedly went electric. He had a job, you see. He had the money to buy a vicious-looking instrument with three pickups and a tremolo arm. Furthermore his best friend and neighbour, Bill Darby, purchased a full drum kit.

Allan and I followed suit. We also bought electric guitars. We joined Stewart and Bill, and formed *Three's Company*, a band that sounded pretty rough and got us into lots of trouble when we played Animals and Them songs at parties and church functions.

Meanwhile, the Quick Brothers band had evaporated. The drummer, Harry Dustin evolved into Harry Young, a singer/frontman. He formed a damn good unit called *Harry Young & the Intriguers*. They had first class equipment and were remarkably professional. We supported them once.

Around this time, the most popular church group was a folk trio called *The Ramblin' Strings*, ie. Dave Hall, Kevin Weir and Alwyn Backhouse.

Harry Young and Sabbath, formed after the Intriguers

Dave Hall was said to be the church's 'best guitarist'. We often saw them performing at church venues.

Although Allan and I were a close-knit twosome at the core of *Three's Company*, Stewart was no passenger. He was almost the bandleader. I don't know what possessed him to team up with us. He had a reputation to lose! Stewart was older than us. He got all the gigs. He had the best equipment. And he was also lead singer. It was Stewart who sang *Irene*, not me. He was the first person to sing any of my songs before an audience. Our crowning moment as *Three's Company* was the Inter-Sydney Church Youth Rally called 'Fanfare'.

Held every three months, about 800 young people converged on the Ashfield Town Hall from all over Sydney. Tony Roy was there, chaperoning his 15-year old cousin Robbie (Robyn) Roy. All *The Rejects* were there, as was the rest of my class. Genna was almost certainly up the back, watching. Louis Rao was there, with his newly formed band

– Colin Chestnut and John Fry. Everyone was there. But Robert Wolfgramm was not. He was attending Lilydale High School, on the outskirts of Melbourne.

Dressed in identical blue velvet shirts, with 'long hair', three electric guitars and Charlie (Charles) Lowe on drums (because Bill couldn't make it), that Saturday night *Three's Company* performed two songs before 800 church kids. First, Stewart sang the Byrds song, *Turn Turn Turn* (with Allan harmonising) then Allan soloed the Rolling Stones' song, *Lady Jane*. Two girls - our girlfriends - screamed. When I turned up at school the following Monday, I thought Louis would say how great we were. Instead he said the local Church Conference had convened and banned our kind of music from all subsequent events. Louis was angry because that meant his band was shut down too. Anyway, I felt we'd probably peaked, we'd made our point and I was getting tired of the whole church-band thing.

So I sold my *Jason* electric guitar, bought an acoustic *Maton* guitar and concentrated on writing songs, alas - not too successfully. I could never replicate the success of *Irene*. Every song I wrote sounded the same. Over the next two years, 1968-69, I seldom played guitar. I concentrated on writing poems and lyrics. And precisely when I was winding down, the church's 'young' music started winding up.

In 1969, Byron Gilmour and I attended a *Town Criers* gig in Newcastle. The Criers had enjoyed lots of hits, most notably a cover version of *Everlasting Love*, which made the Top 10. That night, Byron and I were simply part of the audience. We didn't know anyone. Yet within six years, lead guitarist Sam Dunnin (Melamed) would become a cornerstone of my musical life. And in time, singer Barry Smith would be a friend to Robert.

The big event - I suppose - in Australian church Rock music circa 1969, was that Brian Patterson had walked out of the successful pop band, *The Executives* and joined the church. At last, the church could boast a real Rock n Roll scalp! While Allan, Clayton and I probably weren't too interested in the Executives, we liked Brian in his previous band, *Tony Worsely and the Blue Jays*, with terrific hits like *Just A Little*

Bit! Around this time I ran into Dave Caldwell at a church function.

Robert Wolfgramm (who was raised in Fiji) had been boarding at the Caldwell house when I knew him back in 1965. So I asked Uncle Dave about him and Uncle Dave replied that Robert was learning jazz chords and writing songs. Indeed, Dave's son Ivan frequently performed Robert's songs and 'if only I'd come inside the church, instead of hanging around outside', I'd hear Ivan sing Robert's song, *Come Just As You Are*.

Furthermore, Robert had formed a Rock band, which visually resembled the *Jimi Hendrix Experience* (1) because there were three of them, and (2) because of Robert's Afro hairstyle. There it was - a photograph - passed to me by Ivan - though I had no way of knowing what they sounded like, nor who the other band members were?

In 1970 I was expelled from Avondale College for publishing undesirable poetry. Maybe they didn't like it because at the close of 1969, I started my own stand at Sydney's Domain from which I sold editions of my poems titled *Rags*. Maybe they didn't like that I'd joined forces with the Dada poet, John the Magnificent.

Maybe the whole thing sounded crazy to the ill-tempered college president, Dr Gordon McDowell who expelled me, leaving me to spend 1970 in Sydney, away from Robbie - seeing bands like Tully, light shows by Ellis D Fogg, poetry readings by Robert Adamson, Saturday nights at PACT Folk and meeting Martin Sharp at the Yellow House. It was a good year for me to be living in Sydney.

One day, while bashing my guitar at the Domain, with John the Magnificent blowing random notes from his crazy harmonica, I looked up and there at the back of our crowd was Genna Levitch. He was studying dentistry and I knew he wrote poems. So, after John and I finished our routine, I invited Genna to get up and read.

This poetry stuff was very spontaneous, but a Sunday afternoon Domain session required holding a show together for maybe 2-3 hours in front of an audience. Not a polite church audience, but a real one. Quickly I realised that to make the Rags Stand work needed an 'act' that could occasionally bring everything back to earth, because I simply couldn't hold a show together on Dada poetry alone. I couldn't be 'out there' all the time, I needed to catch my breath and return to something structured, before going 'off' again.

So I asked Stewart if he was interested in performing and he said he was. We formed a trio - Dallas Lewis/lead vocals, Stewart/vocals & 12-string guitar, and me/6-string guitar, writing lots of words and - with Stewart's help - some of the music.

Unlike *Three's Company* - this time around the wheel, there was nothing particularly shocking about us. We weren't electric, we didn't use drums, yes - we had long hair (but by now everyone else had even longer hair). So Dallas, Stewart and I played parties, hospitals, folk venues and we were regulars at the 20-30 Club, a church venue for young adults.

At church concerts, *The Rambling Strings* were still the top act. But by now there were lots of other good players too. Carl Needham and Dave McMahon were jazz bassists in their respective bands. Plus there were always lots of Judds: Jan Judd, Bruce Judd, somewhere in the production zone Warren Judd - and probably even more Judds that I can't recall. Then there were soloists, like Lester Silver, Andy Vidler and Dave Smiley Martin. There were lots more performers too, some of whom were pretty good.

There seemed to be lots of energy around Christian youth culture in 1970. The Jesus Revolution was a *Time* magazine cover story. And everyone was talking about shows like *Superstar* and *Godspell.*

In 1970, Harry Young and the Sabbath were creeping up the pop charts. In 1971 they peaked at #7 with *Wheat in the Field*, but no one at church really noticed. They didn't care, Harry & his Sabbath weren't part of their circle any more.

Robbie and I were engaged now. When I returned to College in 1971, despite *The Rejects, Three's Company* and the Domain, I was a nothing-guitarist. I saw myself as a Chess player, a card sharp and a bit of a poet.

And then, while hanging around the entrance of Watson Hall, way after everyone else had enrolled for the college year, in walked Robert Wolfgramm, carrying a suitcase and a nylon-stringed guitar.

'What are you doing here?' I asked, surprised and hoping he'd remember me.

'Theology', he shrugged.

The band known as *Southern Lights* or *Passport*, (depending whom you ask). The photograph was taken after a recording session (not a Galilee session). It was an important session because it was a key catalyst for the album *Persecution Games*.

3
It Was 1964

Stewart Walker

On reflection, I was probably one of the first Adventist youth to introduce a guitar into church functions and main services.

Stewart and his cutaway guitar

It was 1964. Sci-fi program *The Outer Limits* and the *Dick Van Dyke Show* were popular weekly programs on our monochrome analogue television. The annual Bathurst 1000 at Mount Panorama was called the *Armstrong 500* and a Ford Cortina GT driven by Bob Jane won the race that year.

The Beatles visited Sydney in June and for me, 2UE was the 'in' station, where the Top 40 song chart was promoted and played. The '2SM Good Guys' - Bob Rogers, Mad Mel and Mike Walsh were other popular announcers if a change on the radio dial was needed. And I was 16 going on 17.

Each week, music shops handed out a printed sheet by radio stations 2UE and 2SM listing the Top 20 or 40 most popular songs and recording artists during the week based on record sales and song requests. If we didn't already know from the radio, this 'bible' would inform us who was No 1, for how many weeks and which single vinyl record to buy, (even though the flip side was usually a dud).

A small range of paperback booklets with titles such as *Songster Hit Parade*, *Leeds Top 50 Songsters* and *Boomerang Songster Book* were also sold at the music shops and for one shilling (or later, 15 cents) one would obtain the words to about 50 current and popular songs such as *Hey Paula* and *Ramblin' Rose*. These books were numbered rather than dated but were updated every month or so with the latest song lyrics as the hit parades changed. They were my first recollection of an inexpensive way to find the correct words of 'acceptable' songs to play on the guitar because sheet music was more expensive (usually one shilling per song). And who needed sheet music when one couldn't read music and played all the songs in the same key! Improvising became a lifesaver for me on many occasions.

Throughout 1964 I was still teaching myself the guitar, but I'm getting a bit ahead of myself...

Going back to 1960, my family migrated to Australia from England and we met up again with my cousin Lowell and his family who had migrated the previous year. Having being taught the piano back in England for four years, and later scratching out scales on the violin for some months, I had a basic knowledge of music and chords, even though I still struggled to read music and defied my music teacher by preferring to play from memory.

Once in Australia I had no desire to continue piano lessons, but I still had no problems listening to a tune and picking it out on the piano keys. It was usually in the scale of C or G but most modern songs of that era only consisted of three or four basic chords, which for me were easy to play even if the harmony wasn't quite right.

As we didn't have a piano at home, I was thrilled to be given a very old Spanish guitar from an aunt in England. Accompanying it was a basic book of guitar chords, and this was all I needed to find the fingering on the frets for my favourite chords of C, G and F and I built on these.

That guitar was always kept at home because it was fragile and cracked, and it didn't quite carry the musicians' 'look' as seen with the pop groups on TV. But I cut my teeth on this instrument teaching myself the rudiments of guitar playing and I became quite attached to it over the next four years.

In 1964 I branched out and bought my next guitar, an acoustic cutaway style that I sheepishly carried around in a brown calico bag with drawstring because I couldn't afford a case. Now *this* was a guitar that I could be seen with in public, with shiny metal parts that I could polish, modern design and polished lacquered wood. Even if it didn't have a brand name printed on it, I could carry it with pride to venues where I performed.

Because I enjoyed playing the guitar, it was inevitable that in time, I would teach and play with Lowell, my only cousin. We had always enjoyed each other's company and 1964 was when it all started. Lowell had also had years of piano tuition, so our love and understanding of music were somewhat on the same level even though he could read music better than I. The first hint that we would be drawn together musically was when we would 'perform' at family parties. There were several of these family gatherings and one I recall was early in 1964 when the two of us performed a Beatles Show, usually miming the songs and acting like clowns. We were the main entertainment at family parties, which to me was pride mixed with a form of escapism from the usual parental regulations.

During these months, I sat down with Lowell and taught him the basics of playing the guitar. Due to his past years of experience on the piano, he quickly picked up the chords and other techniques shone and he soon started developing his own style of music and was keen enough to purchase his own guitar and amplifier. These were fun carefree days in our teens when we could make disastrous mistakes and the family would still applaud and we would still proudly accept credit no matter how bad we were.

I was one of a growing number of Adventist young people who played guitar and during 1964/65 I was also part of the Wahroonga Youth Choir. As well as singing, I was chosen to play the solo instrumental break in the hymn *How Great Thou Art* as part of the choirs' repertoire.

Most times we performed that hymn using an amplifier we borrowed from the church's Conference Office and by then, I had converted my acoustic cutaway guitar to electric. I achieved this by attaching a pick-up bar unceremoniously screwed under the strings. I also bought (from the local hardware store) a copper door hinge on which I glued on one side a wad of foam padding and covered it in a velvet cloth. I then welded on a metal arm that I attached to one side of the hinge. This rather crude invention was to get that special guitar 'mute' sound when I raised the arm hinge to wedge under the strings, which incidentally worked! The guitar solo with the choir was my first introduction to playing my electric guitar in front of total strangers at many different churches and functions with the choir and although to me it sounded crappy, I felt I had taken my first steps into a new world.

My music of choice was Country and Western. I preferred slow songs and, as I had a soft voice, Country and Western ballads had the desired rhythm and emotion that I felt I could bond with. Also, it was much easier to strum out a chord rather than pick strings, especially when I had no teacher to help master that art and, learning only by memorizing a tune, I started learning to strum chords to such favourites as *Cool Water* and *Old Shep*. Our church at Guildford held regular Saturday night social evenings, usually commemorating various events such as 21st Birthdays, engagements, farewells, etc, and these two songs were always favourite requests, even though one was sung by the "evil" Elvis! (He was smart though, he would stagger his Rock and Roll gyrating hits with an occasional hymn such as *Peace in the Valley* or ballads such as *Can't Help Falling in Love* to win the acceptance of both old and new generations.)

I would usually be accompanied by Erwin Barrington on his ukulele and, between the two of us, we had similar musical harmonies - enough to keep the folk happy. Mind you, tunes such as *Running Bear* had a bit more of a beat and took a while to be accepted. I wonder if anyone realized that almost all our songs were played in the same key!

On reflection (I was unaware at the time), I was probably one of the first Adventist youth to introduce a guitar into church functions and main services. The guitar had been considered a questionable instrument by the older generation as it had gained its recent popularity through Rock and Roll music and I could sense that the instrument was frowned upon when appearing anywhere near a church.

During that year, I attended Merrylands High School and I regularly took my guitar to school and jammed with other musicians, learning chords and songs. Being a public school, we had a music room where we could express ourselves with our instruments outside school hours and guitars were all the rage because groups such as the Beatles and the Rolling Stones were starting to become popular on the radio airwaves. As a result it was cool to own a guitar even if one couldn't play and we always had a flood of girls hanging around no matter how bad the sound was.

In March 1966, I decided to visit my favourite music shop, Bloche's Music Merrylands, and I bought my first amplifier which would see me through the next few years. I wanted something to last, have quality and the ability to hold more than one instrument, so I chose a Vadis amplifier for 160 pounds which I had to pay off over a few weeks before finally collecting it. To me, it was a cumbersome beast but a joy to behold as it came in two sections, the top with all the valves, dial controls and switches, with the capacity for four input jacks, plus an echo chamber and vibrato controlled by two foot switches. The bottom, much larger section, had 2 x 12inch bass speakers and sub woofers. Undoubtedly, with such a unit, my playing could only improve...so I thought. It wasn't long after that I realized my guitar didn't really suit the amplifier in looks or sound, so shortly after I was back at the music shop purchasing a solid body electric guitar with a real guitar case included.

By now, Lowell was quite confident in playing the guitar with me, and we recruited another guitar playing friend of Lowell's named Allan Broadhurst to join us as a singer and guitarist. This would be cool I thought as Allan had the long blonde hair and looks to attract the girls, and of course, as we practiced, we realized we had to have a name to identify our group, and the name *Three's Company* was born. Later, a good friend of mine named Bill, took an interest in joining us and as he had no previous knowledge of playing musical instruments, I suggested drums - as a drummer would complete the band. Bill bought a drum kit, started taking lessons and we practiced as a group whenever we could. One would have assumed that with a fourth player, the name of the group would have to be changed, but the name *Three's Company* remained, begging the question 'if three's company, does that mean four's a crowd?'

We made noise, lots of noise, and somewhere in that noise there were the recognised sounds of the occasional song. We practiced wherever we could and many times, as we still lived at home, it would be at our parents' house. In our garage at Guildford, little kids would gather outside from surrounding streets to listen. At Lowell's place in Turramurra, we would play on the back verandah overlooking the bush, and the music was so loud that kids would follow the sound through the bush from over the other side of the valley in St Ives to hang over the back fence to see and hear us practice.

After seeing the Beatles and the Bee Gees with their similar suits and hairstyles, we also figured we needed a gimmick to bond us together as a group, and in April 1966, Bill gave me a royal blue velvet shirt for my birthday. That seemed to be the key and we all ended up buying the same distinctive shirt. Perhaps, the feeling was that such an outfit would reinforce our group, and our sound would improve and we would gain popularity, so we practiced more than ever, whenever and wherever we could. Our problem was mainly distance with two of the band living on one side of Sydney and two on the other side and no ready means of transport at our disposal. However, this did not deter us and we would phone each other with song suggestions and practice our individual parts in our own styles alone during the week and try to turn the result into a tune on the weekends, with sometimes questionable results.

With Allan and Lowell now singers in the group, they had their own distinctive style of songs which were leaning more towards a heavier/louder/swing beat, almost a type of Garage Rock style of featuring *Gloria* and *Mystic Eyes* by a popular group called Them, an Irish band with a singer named Van Morrison. I still preferred to sing the slower love/ ballad type arrangements that I could put feeling into. Although I still performed in all songs, I left the singing of the more lively numbers to them. Because the popular music of the day accepted by youth embraced both categories, I felt comfortable branching out from the older Country and Western ballads that pleased the elderly relatives and church folk to more modern ballads sung by the likes of the Bee Gees, Roy Orbison, Peter and Gordon, Simon and Garfunkel and even Elvis Presley.

Now we had the use of two guitar amplifiers and, as one of them had an adjustable echo chamber, we took advantage of this by running our microphone through it whenever we sang. None of us had ever received any formal singing training, so by singing through the echo chamber, the quality of our voices improved dramatically. Notes seemed to hang on and harmonies lingered, a much better sound than we could have otherwise produced without the marvels of modern electronics.

Over the next couple of years, the group performed at various functions both private and social events run by the church. By this time, other group bands mainly made up of church teens started to follow suit. Again mainly guitars and drums, but occasionally one would have a different approach. I recall a group led by Greg Parr playing at a social function in Concord Church Hall. His group was more jazz orientated and included a saxophone, an instrument that hadn't weathered the criticisms and baptisms of fire in church functions as our electric guitars, amplifiers and drums had done over the years. Unfortunately, the older folk in the audience didn't appreciate the music or style and Greg's band was stopped after the first couple of songs.

Our group was luckier at the functions we played at and soldiered on despite the occasional air of disapproval from elderly church folk who hadn't heard us before or just never approved of guitars and modern music. We played at parties and church functions sometimes sharing the stage with other groups who sounded a bit better than us, but we persevered. Occasionally we were in such demand that we had back-to-back performances on the same day at different venues which gave us the warm feeling that perhaps we were progressing in some way.

4
Brass Bands, Other Bands

Robert Wolfgramm

I started writing songs in 1968 as a 16-year old boarder at Lilydale Adventist Academy.

Robert dressed for the 1965 Anzac Day Dawn Service and March

The first cornettists in the *Sydney Advent Brass Band* were occasionally led by a bloke whose name I can't remember, but it was something like Larry Bird, a name like that. He was a handsome man, a smooth dresser with an air of cool about him - this was 1964-66 - like he might have been a nightclub jazz muso who happened to be an Adventist.

Anyway, when he sat in with the band, he seemed to lift everyone's spirits and our performances accordingly. The band members paid him enormous respect and positively glowed when he fronted up. In pieces that called for an improvisation, it was he who invariably stood up behind his music stand and took them. He was friendly and had the confidence of someone who knew what they were doing on their instrument.

The rest of the time, practices could be stodgy. Hard work and a lot to learn. It was at band practice that I eventually figured out what key signatures were. I thought everything was in the key of C until then and I oompah-ed along accordingly no matter how many sharps or flats were posted at the beginning of each stave. For me, if it was a note on the first space of the stave, if was F – first finger on the first valve. Until my colleague on his bigger B-flat pointed to the sharp sign and gestured with his middle finger on the second valve – ah, I learned F-sharp. And so until I realized what a donkey I'd been and no wonder the band sounded decidedly flat at times – especially on the quiet numbers.

Well, I'm glad to say, it wasn't until I'd learned the differences between sharps and flats and why they mattered, that I was allowed to join in the public performances of the band. And when I did, I took to chromatic scales like a fish to water. I would sit in Uncle Dave Caldwell's green school van that we used to practice in, and I'd run through every piece I could play and transpose them by sight into all of the 12 semi-tonal keys - to make sure I was not going to get caught out mixing up naturals, sharps and flats ever again.

The band members were an interesting subculture. The leader and conductor for the most part was a man named Norm Trood. (I think that was him.) There was a tenor horn player with an impish grin and he seemed to be the funny man of the outfit – always cracking jokes and keeping spirits up when the going got heavy. He had an equally funny sidekick from school, a ginger-headed, smart-talking thin fellow,

Dickie Chapman (not his real name), who also played tenor, or baritone or euphonium. He always came along in school uniform or sometimes with denim jeans instead of school trousers. Dickie told us a joke one night that has stuck with me for some reason and it concerned a devout man he and his mates played a trick on at Avondale College one night.

The joke was that the man was in the habit of kneeling at the base of particular tree to pray in the evenings and that Dickie and his friends decided to climb the very same tree and hide while he did this. As the man prayed Dickie whispered down from his perch in solemn voice answers to the man's prayers as if God himself were giving a direct and immediate response. According to Dickie, the man was not only taken in, but scared out of his wits and he ran from the place in haste. It sounds cruel now but I remember it being very funny when Dickie told it to us outside during a break in band practice. I was about 13 and Dickie must have been about 17. There were about five of us from school band who had made it into the big band at that stage (and who heard the joke).

Charlie Lowe on trombone was another. He was a cool guy too, oozing charm and with a hip swagger to go with it. And a very nice guy. Barnsey Butler on cornet was there too. It was his Dad, Lance, who collected us all in his Valiant sedan and carted us from Sydney's North Shore to Strathfield where the rehearsal was held. Lance was a very nice man, always kind and approachable. His son Barnes was in my year perhaps, but a motor-head who - with Charlie and Dickie - mostly talked about cars, V8s, torque and race-tracks. It was among them at band practice I first heard about 'double de-clutching' and stuff like that.

The practices were held in rooms at the rear of the Church's Greater Sydney headquarters in Strathfield. The chairs and stands were set up by whoever arrived first and that wasn't us very often, as coming from the North Shore was not as close as coming up from the south or Inner West where others lived. It was a good discipline going to practice and learning music at the shoulders of these older men. Some were mechanical practical chaps, others were bookish clerical types and others seemed to be church workers from a variety of occupational backgrounds. None of them had what were then considered migrant surnames – that is, none of the band was Mediterranean, Baltic, Balkan or Southern European. There were no Greeks, Italians, Poles, Egyptians, Turks, Bulgarians, Serbs, Spanish, Swedes or even French – although there was a guy named Beauilleau who might have had French ancestors, otherwise he was as 'Aussie' as Holden.

And Wolfgramm of course was German, but as far as the band was concerned I was 'Fiji' to start with. That's what they called me. That nickname soon evolved into the more Japanese 'Fuji' for some reason, but my school band mates never called me that, I was always 'Shorty' to them. When other band members spoke to me it was, 'Got that Fuji?' or 'Fuji's ready' or 'You tell 'em Fuji' or something like that. I never minded. I grew up in Fiji with a family nickname (Smokey). And my darkness of complexion led one of my uncles to call me 'Charcoal'.

Our repertoire at rehearsals was always a selection of hymns. *Abide With Me* became a favourite, not just because I mastered it early on, but because its slow solemn progression from sadness to triumph moves the spirit no matter who performs it choral, brass, or orchestra. Marches were always on the menu too and some were easier than others. *Colonel Bogey's* was not my favourite despite it being popular at the time. The *BB and CF* was wonderful with its crashing descending bass scales. I liked *Thin Red Line* too. They took a while to master, but they worked well with the band. A concert piece I enjoyed was *In a Persian Market*. Somewhere in this thing we had to sing 'Bhaksheesh, bhaksheesh, allah' – hilarious.

As well practice the tunes, we also practiced marching. We used the Strathfield SDA High School ground for it. On Sundays we assembled and marched up and down, wheeling left and right and back into ourselves. It was tiring. Our march pieces were all part of preparation for ANZAC Day 1965 – the 50th anniversary of the Gallipoli landing and big occasion right across Australia and New Zealand.

We marched in the Sydney procession – a huge occasion that was televised live. Some of the band members hoped that we would get on the screen, but of course none of us would know. I can't remember if we did, but it was quite an experience – my left shoe was heeled by the bloke behind me and I dragged my left foot most of the way up George Street to Hyde Park. But the gathering was huge. Veterans by the thousands turned out from both World Wars. We started out from Circular Quay. The word went around that the marchers were so numerous that some bands including us were asked to march twice just to accommodate them all.

In Easter 1966 we competed in the Australian national band championships. We were only good enough to be in D grade but hoped to be good enough to be promoted to C. Our performance in the Sydney Town Hall was OK, but I don't know if we made it up into C. There were dozens of bands and it was very competitive.

1968-1970

I started writing songs in 1968 as a 16-year old boarder at Lilydale Adventist Academy in the outer eastern, semi-rural suburbs of Melbourne. I wrote them on borrowed guitars. I'd learned a little bit of guitar from Uncle Dave, Lowell Tarling, and Louis Rao while at Strathfield the previous year. I'm still writing songs and still learning to play the guitar - are these things ever mastered?

In Australia, early in 1968, PM Harold Holt disappeared and was replaced by John Gorton. Holt went for a swim on Cheviot Beach on the Mornington Peninsula south east of Melbourne and never came out of the surf. He simply disappeared. All kinds of conspiracy theories came to the fore, but the one that lawyers spread was that Holt committed suicide because he was gay and was about to be outed. That wouldn't rate an eyebrow raise today, but back in the 1960s, such a revelation would have dynamited his career.

In the US that year there were race riots, uni sit-ins (ie. occupation of university space by protesting students), and flag and draft card burnings. Things were even worse in France as radicals upped the ante on their campuses. In Czechoslovakia, the Soviets invaded to put the reform-minded president, Mr Dubcek, in his place. At the Chicago Democratic Convention in 1968, right-wing Mayor Daley gave orders to 'shoot to kill' protesters who disrupted the occasion.

In pop culture, Eldridge Cleaver's book *Soul On Ice* was a sobering journey into the experience of a young black American radical. Carlos Castaneda's *Teachings of Don Juan* were fictitious wisdom passed off as anthropological fact. But fact or fiction, it didn't matter to a drug-addled hippie.

Songs that hit in 1968 were *Both Sides Now* (Judy Collins), *Mrs Robinson* (Simon & Garfunkel), *Galveston* (Glen Campbell), *Spinning Wheel* (Blood Sweat and Tears), *Jumping Jack Flash* (Rolling Stones), *Hurdy Gurdy Man* (Donovan), *Windmills Of Your Mind* (Dusty Springfield) and *Little Green Apples* (OC Smith). In film, Stanley Kubrick's *2001: A Space Odyssey* was worth seeing. Guitar sales skyrocketed in the US from $35m (in 1960) to $130m (in 1968) – the rest of the world soon followed that trend.

While Yippies were making headlines as absurdist hippies with a political agenda, I was more interested in owning the Beatles' so-called *White Album* and *Magical Mystery Tour* (an EP record). And in owning Led Zeppelin's first self-titled album; country-blues rockers, Canned Heat's *Goin' Up The Country*, Creedence Clearwater Revival's *Suzie Q*, Jimi Hendrix's *Axis: Bold As Love*, Cream's *Sunshine of Your Love* and *White Room*, Vanilla Fudge's *You Keep me Hanging On*, Iron Butterfly's *In-a-gadda-da-vidda'*, Steppenwolf's *Born to Be Wild*, Janis Joplin's *Cheap Thrills*, Traffic's *Feeling Alright*, The Who's *Magic Bus*, and Pink Floyd's *Ummagumma*.

And more interested in winning the Warburton Talent Quest. With an electric bass guitar and three amplifiers leased from John Robinson's music shop in Croydon (in Melbourne's outer-eastern suburbs), we formed an unnamed group. I worked out the Beatles *Daytripper* as an instrumental and we practised. On the Saturday night of the talent quest, our school-aged fans in the audience screamed their way through our performance and for an encore such that the show compére (Robert Parr) let us do it again. We won the night with more counted votes than there were persons in the audience!

But the highlight of 1968 was going to my first 'disco' in Melbourne, Piccadilly's, in Ringwood Town Hall. The venue became that each Saturday night. My Academy mate, Neil Raymond, was hip to the beat and invited me off the campus to his home one weekend so we could see this hot new band he raved about called *The Party Machine*, who were appearing at Piccadillys.

They were good, but Lobby Loyde was better. There were a lot of girls there and they were dancing, usually together, while the boys and their boyfriends stood back and around the rim of the hall. Like most of them I was terrified a girl might actually ask me to dance. The best defence against this possibility was to look as mean as a young 16-year old black kid from the Pacific could.

I looked at the parade of bands taking the stage and wondered how hard it could be to play rock, get famous and make some money making young girls swoon?

EMMAUS/NINE MILES FROM HOME

Lyrics and Music – Robert Wolfgramm 1969

G C D G
Nine miles from home on a lonely country road
C D G
I kinda get the feeling like I'm lost, all alone
C D G
In my confusion, a stranger tells me all
Burning feeling down inside
C D G
I want to hear more
F C Bb C G
Truth lies inside, is that what he said?
F C Bb C G
What are the answers to the questions in my head?
Dm7/9 –Dm – Gm - Gm7/9
Emmaus
Emmaus
Emmaus
Emmaus

Robert: I worked this one out on one of many hitch-hiking trips between Melbourne and Sydney on the Hume Highway. Most of it while waiting for a ride at the Canberra turn-off outside Yass. It was late afternoon, getting chilly, and desperate for a ride, the best thing that took my mind off the uncertainty was to work out songs from Bible stories I'd been reading. Never performed publicly, but for a few times at Peter McDougall's Bible studies during the 70s. Peter liked the way the song started, but thought it 'got lost toward the end bit'. I recorded a version of it in the late 80s at my Upper Ferntree Gully home with Neale Farnell (bass) and Lee Davidson (guitar and drums).

5
Uncle Bill Wolfgramm

Lowell Tarling

Bill Wolfgramm & His Islanders recorded South Sea Rhythm which has the distinction of being the first 33 rpm album to be pressed in New Zealand.

Bill playing his regular spot at Papatoe RSA

Back in 1971, when Robert told me his Uncle Bill played in a band, I didn't catch its significance. After all, my father played in a dance band too, which he gave up when he became a Seventh-day Adventist. So when Robert told me about his uncle, that's all I thought he meant – that he knocked out dance tunes in some local venue somewhere. Many years after that conversation, I realised Uncle Bill Wolfgramm was much more than that.

In those days, Acid Rock was in vogue and islander music wasn't. I wasn't keen on either. I was more interested in Leonard Cohen, Bob Dylan and Randy Newman. However, I liked the ukulele instrument because I really enjoyed Tiny Tim at his 1968 peak. Everybody did. *Tiptoe Through the Tulips* reached No 7 in the US charts and his first album *God Bless Tiny Tim* hit No 17. But when I was having this conversation with Robert in 1971, in a bull paddock somewhere beyond the SHF Factory on the Avondale College campus, Tiny Tim's career had dropped without a trace, and it would be a decade before I'd find him again.

Some time after the release of *Persecution Games*, and because of my interest in Tiny, I chased down other versions of a song Tiny sang called *The Hukilau*.

That's when I found Bill Wolfgramm & his Islanders had recorded the song on an LP record that was a hit in New Zealand in the 1950s. Yes - Robert had told me about his Uncle Bill, but the penny didn't drop until maybe 1995.

Strangely, in 1983 because of a radio interview, Allan Broadhurst and I were walking through the record library at ABC Radio-Bega. The female interviewer whisked Allan away, leaving me alone in a room full of LP records. And right there, without touching anything or searching, smack before my eyes in an open file was the album *Island Sounds of the South Pacific* by Bill Wolfgramm & His Islanders.

'I could steal this,' I thought. 'I could steal this and send it to Robert. Bega radio won't miss it!'

The original line-up of the pre-Islanders band included three brothers – Robert's father (piano), another uncle and Bill the genius. 'There must have been a tiff,' Robert speculated, because his father wasn't included when Uncle Bill created the Islanders.

During the 80s my interest in Tiny Tim time-travelled me back to the music of the 30s and 40s, after which I got into the history of the ukulele and I bought Jim Beloff's book *The Ukulele*. I even bought a uke – not to play – but to follow what was being written about. That's where I discovered Eddie Kamae and rediscovered Uncle Bill Wolfgramm.

Uncle Bill reminds me of Jimi Hendrix in the way he enters a song

– *Move over Rover, and let Jimi take over!* – Uncle Bill 'arrives' like that, and the song lifts off from there.

Uncle Bill started playing the steel guitar at 19 years old. At age 23, Wolfgramm immigrated to New Zealand where he formed the band. *Bill Wolfgramm and His Rhythm* was a big draw card on the live music scene. Uncle Bill was a major recording star in New Zealand during the 1950s.

In those years, when the transition from 78 rpm records to 33 rpm records was taking place, Bill Wolfgramm & His Islanders recorded *South Sea Rhythm* which has the distinction of being the first 33rpm album to be pressed in New Zealand. He carried on recording up to the 1970s and was active into the early 1990s. He died in 2003. I looked Uncle Bill up on the Internet which proudly announces that he is the uncle of recording artist Nani Wolfgramm, who I don't know anything about.

Uncle Bill is also the uncle of the Wolfgramm family in the USA who formed the band *The Jets*. Like the Osmonds, the Jets are a big Mormon family band. The original line-up comprised, LeRoy, Eddie, Eugene, Haini, Kathi, Elizabeth and Moana - all Wolfgramms. And it doesn't end there. More recent line-ups have included at least 10 other family members.

In the mid-late 80s the original band had five Top 10 singles on Billboard most notably the 1986 *Crush On You* which peaked at #3 in July 1986. But we didn't notice them much in Australia – well, I didn't. In 1997, American popster Britney Spears covered the Jets' *You Got It All* though I can't say I really noticed her either.

I was more interested in yet another Wolfgramm family band - Robert and Ag's daughters - the *Wolfgramm Sisters*, Kelly, Talei and Eliza.

Readers must have noticed their regular appearances on the TV show *RockWiz*. It's worth chasing down on youtube, especially (for my tastes) *When I Need You* with Leo Sayer and *Tin Soldier* with Tim Rogers. The Wolfgramm Sisters have release two CDs, plus singles, and appear on countless recordings with bands I don't know like Little Birdie, etc.

One time Robbie and I went to Melbourne's Crown Casino to see the *British Rock Symphony*, starring Eric Burdon, Thelma Houston and Glenn Shorrock. Even though the Wolfgramm Sisters were in the backing band, I didn't get to meet Eric Burdon. But I kissed Thelma Houston's hand.

Back to that paddock in 1971, Robert talked to me about islander music, which was much less fashionable then than it is now.

Each February, Katoomba NSW (where Robbie and I live) holds a UkeFest known as the *Blue Mountains Ukulele Festival*. Bands – I mean, 70-piece 'ukestras' travel from as far afield as Newcastle, Gosford and all over NSW to perform here.

I am exhibiting my collection of signed Tiny Tim posters.

And, one coffee shop has requested a burn of the CD I have of Bill Wolfgramm & His Islanders.

Kelly, Talei and Eliza

6
The Road to Mackay and Back

Robert Wolfgramm

We were the church's Sixties Generation making our mark at the Pacific church's preeminent educational institution.

I think it was Jude Burnett's idea to visit her in Mackay Qld during Easter 1971. I was mildly open to the dare, but Ivy Woo was all for it and talked me into it.

Jude was part of an arty group, Avondale College bohemians, which defined itself by self-attachment and peer acceptance. Everyone in it was smart, clever, hip or intellectual in some artistic way that most Adventists at the time were not. A symbolic indication of this can be seen in the prominence given to us in that year's *Jacaranda 1971*, the annual College journal of the year's achievements, enrolments and notable events. We were the church's Sixties Generation making our mark at the Pacific church's preeminent educational institution.

Lowell was the poetic centre of a group that included Julene, Ivy, Robbie, Nomi, Harriet and the young gay men, Dale and Geoff. I was at the guitar end of things.

But Lowell connected all of us having interests in English literature, art, music, poetry and writing. He'd had works published in the church's periodicals. We were in awe of his gifts. Julene was as brainy as anyone got and played trombone and bluesy-jazzy recorder. Ivy was Hawaiian-Chinese and beautiful, having on occasion babysat for Quincy Jones and his actor wife, Peggy Lipton. She possessed, as a gift from them, a Martin guitar which she loaned me a lot of the time. Robbie was a former Lilydale student I didn't really know, but she knew a lot about macramé and other fine arts. Nomi was the daughter of a university lecturer in psychology and had a wit and humour that had me intrigued and all of us laughing. Harriet was somewhat aloof, an image of what I imagined a famous English crime-fiction writer might look like. Dale was Lowell's roommate, privately courageous, impressively knowledgeable and always welcoming. Geoff was camp, a sharp dresser whose body language was thought 'sissy'. Jude was a blonde, long legged hippie from North Queensland. Occasionally there were others on the fringes of our group like Anthea Nicholls, Patrice Mitchell and Sharron Kennedy.

Anyway, when the fortnight Easter break came around, Jude left for Mackay by coach or plane and left it to Ivy and I to find our own way up to her. We set out hitchhiking.

By evening of the first day, we were at Tweed Heads crossing the NSW border into Queensland. The night was long and cold, and rides difficult, but we managed to find our way the next morning in the north of Brisbane in a station wagon heading to Rockhampton. It was not a great feeling waking up at a point in that ride and overhearing the driver suggesting to Ivy in the front seat that I was baggage she could do without. About 30 hours after we first set out, we made it into Mackay on an overcast afternoon, past cane fields, over railway lines, and finally into the backblocks of the sugar country capital where we met Jude and her Mum. They were as amazed as we were that we had made it.

After a day of sitting around doing little except enjoying Jude and her Mum's hospitality, seeing the small city of Mackay, and strumming my guitar, I decided I'd take my leave and hitchhike back to Sydney. It was a slower, lonelier trip, having no pretty Hawaiian girl to attract the eye of hurrying drivers.

Somehow I made it to Rockhampton by mid-afternoon. On the south side of the mining city, I caught a ride with the *Gladstone Gladiators* – a bikie group of three chaps all sitting in the front bench seat of a Holden station wagon. The floor of the back seat area was covered in melting ice and beer. I was welcomed into the back seat and had to put my feet on the driveshaft hump on the floor to keep them dry. And no sooner was I in the car than the three drunk bikies were calling for music, songs, anything that I could play from the radio that they knew and could sing along to.

I was praying feverishly, but immediately began rehearsing in my mind every pop song Lowell and Louis Rao had taught me, every song I had learned at Lilydale, and at Avondale since. But as soon I struck up, they loved it, arms swinging across the windscreen, voices shouting the choruses 'Rollin', rollin' rollin' on a river, dah dah dah dum, dah dah dah dum, dah dah dah dum dum, dah dah dah' followed by whooping and ending with 'you're alright Bob, you're alright ... we like you Bob, you're not a smartarse, you're alright – got another one Bob?'

Sure, I'd reply about to launch for the fifth time into *Get off My Cloud* before they'd cut me off, 'Nah, a beer mate'. 'Sorry' - and I'd have to pass a few more tinnies to the front seat, sure that I was handing over my death sentence to the increasing drunkenness of my three good Samaritans. Their bikes had been confiscated, they told me, and that was why we were all in this station wagon hurtling down the Bruce Highway toward Gladstone from Rocky usually on our side of the road, but often on the other, zig-zagging the lines, me outwardly guitaring and singing and inwardly praying, but everyone deliriously happy in the front seat.

As we approached Gladdy, they told me they were turning off but would help me get a ride from a well-known pub on the crossroad. It was frequented by truckies - 'One of'm will take ya to Brissy Bob, don't worry, we'll get y'ride there mate'. I was reluctant to go inside with my inebriated newfound mates, but they were insistent and I dared not argue. As we pushed through the doors into the main bar, there weren't many there, but a half a dozen were truckies for sure. Their blue singlets contrasted with the bikie denim and leather. 'Anyone of you'z going to Brissy can give our mate Bob a lift?' Silence. 'C'mon fellas, any you'z pooftas going south can help our little mate here?' Silence. 'Where you going?' Townsville, came the answer, then Rocky, then Cairns, and so on around the bar until it was clear that if anyone was going to Brisbane no one was letting on. 'Sorry Bob, none a these f... p... c...s can help ya [silence] ... lyin' bastards'. And with that, they encouraged me to leave and we all did.

I crossed over the highway to the south side of the intersection with nothing but forest and signposts and a quietly lit bar in behind rows of parked semitrailers.

Half an hour or so and dark, a truck wheeled out of the pub's gravel carpark and hissed up beside me. Gladly I jumped in, rejoicing. 'I woulda said yes in there but I was ... y'know...', the truckie admitted smiling. I agreed seeking help with three drunk bikies as mouthpieces was not exactly a good diplomacy technique and explained my position. The truckie was glad for the company. 'I want you to keep me awake' he said. He then asked me to open up a small silver foil pack of yellow and purple pills and to hand him a couple. Taking his bottle of cola, he slammed them down. If my time with the Gladstone Gladiators was bad, this truckie and his rig was not looking promising.

I was soon proved right. The truck was all lit up for our night journey south - except if we hit a particularly bad pothole or bump, at which the headlights would be knocked out for an eternal few seconds. None of which slowed us down, we would simply gun-on into the pitch black without a moon and surrounded by forest, the truckie cursing heaven and everything holy until slamming his fist on the dashboard for the second or third time, whereby the lights would flicker back on.

I was so scared I just prayed harder than when I was in the back seat of the station wagon. I noticed with each dose of pills I handed the truckie, he simply became more nervy and agitated, his eyeballs sticking out on stalks, his gestures jerky and his chatter reduce to rapid-fire machine 'What's up Bob?' he'd ask with a sense of panic in the inflexion. 'Nothing' I'd reassure him.

At one point he reached to adjust his exterior vertical mirror only to send his hand so emphatically into it that it cracked and smashed. Great, I thought, not only on-again-off-again headlights to see what hazards lay ahead, but also no mirror to see what danger might be coming up behind. Lord what are you doing to me? I wondered.

By the first light of day, we miraculously made Brisbane. I'd nodded off to sleep, hungry, but my truckie had somehow no-dozed his way to a truckstop on the northern edge of the Queensland capital. I'd missed Bundaberg, Maryborough, Gympie, and Nambour in the night. But I thanked God I was still in my skin and not a road statistic for the usually perilous Easter toll. Surprisingly, the truckie apologised for the rough trip but I thanked him, was grateful for the lift and wished him well. Within a short while, as the morning traffic was building up, a small one-ton truck pulled up and offered me a lift, The driver, an Indian from Fiji, welcomed me and asked me if I would help him unload his timber at a building site off the highway after which he would deliver me back to a highway intersection. I was wary of his boastful chatter and his growing quiet contempt for what must have seemed to him, my privileged life – that is, attending a tertiary education institution without a care in the world (ie. on a hitch-hiking holiday) while he was grinding out timber deliveries for a living. The more we talked, the bigger the chip on his shoulder grew.

It was only Easter 1971 heck, and my guess was that he was a reluctant exile following Fiji's national independence some six months earlier – an Indian fearful for what post-independence, post-colonialism may lead to in the hands of indigenous political power. By the time we unloaded at his site, he had turned completely against me. When he told me defiantly he would not deliver me as promised to the highway, I was not surprised, just disappointed and angry that he had lived up to a terrible stereotype I had inherited as to the Indian character.

Finding my way back to the Pacific Highway took a few hours. It was lunchtime and I still hadn't eaten since setting out from Mackay a day and half before. But I was buoyed by being south of Brissy and heading down the Pacific Highway to Sydney. Getting through the Gold Coast was not easy – a lot of traffic, yes, but none of it stopping.

Somewhere in Southport I caught up with a hippie New Age girl who smelled as unwashed I was, but was chirpy and friendly and happy to join forces. I wasn't sure if she was straight or high on something, but she had some money and offered to shout me a cuppa – an offer I gladly accepted. On sighting a nearby park, she then said she was tired and wanted to have a sleep if I wouldn't mind minding her things – a couple of billabong bags. Yeah, sure, I replied. As soon as we found a shady spot out of the mid-afternoon sun, I put my head down on one of her bags. I don't know if she slept, but when I woke up, she was gone (*Norwegian Wood*). Walking back to the highway I spotted her a few hundred meters ahead, her thumb out for a ride. I kept my distance and we never saw each other again.

In contrast to my Bruce Highway experiences north of Brisbane, my rides south to Sydney were as pacific as the highway that bears its name. As providence would have it, in the fading light of Murwillumbah, I picked up a truck heading all the way to Sydney and beyond. A single ride is the hope of every hitchhiker and, weakened by lack of sleep and food, I nodded on and off through the north coast of New South Wales cities of Lismore, Grafton, Coffs Harbour, Port Macquarie and Newcastle.

The blur passed from dusk of one day to dawn of the next. By mid-morning and 56 hours after I'd farewelled Ivy and Jude, I hopped gratefully out of the cab of my host truckie, and was soon knocking on the door of my 'brother' Ivan Caldwell's flat in Hornsby.

It was not far from the main shopping mall on the city side of the line. Ivan, fresh out of teacher's college, shared the flat with his sister, my 'sister' Ronnie. They both welcomed me. I can still recall falling onto the carpeted floor of the flat, all clean and fed and sleeping deeply most of the day away.

On waking up in the late afternoon sunlight, Ronnie was smiling still and Ivan was playing his guitar in his room. A visitor came by and left and then Ivan announced he or we had an appointment to sing a 'special item' ie. a song, at a 'Saltshaker' concert that evening - if I wanted to. What song should we do, Ivan wondered. I offered my 13-bar *Jesus Blues No. 2* - otherwise known as *War 'n' Hate 'n' Troubles*. He thought that was good - he'd play rhythm, I'd play lead and sing and we'd see how it went. It went OK I think. Not great, but OK. There was some cheering and applause. The next day, Ivan and Ronnie were kind enough to give me my train fare and a bit of pocket money to get back to Avondale.

When Jude and Ivy returned, Ivy and I were champions. We'd made it on the road Kerouac-like all the way to Mackay - 1200 miles - and I'd made it another 1200 miles back. Added to the half dozen return trips I'd done between Melbourne and Sydney in the three years previous - a bit more than 6000 miles up and down Highway 31 - I'd hitch-hiked at least eight and half thousand miles in total (nearly 14,000 kms) in those formative song-writing years. Without realising it at the time, I'd followed, naively, yet certainly, and out of necessity, in the footsteps of Woody Guthrie and other Beat poet-writers, working out chord progressions, sounds and riffs while waiting for the charity and generosity of strangers to rescue me from being somewhere in between where I'd left, to somewhere else I was heading.

I usually dressed in jeans and a shirt, or t-shirt, with a duffle coat and jumper stuffed into a small airline bag, a guitar and sometimes an umbrella. And a finger (not thumb) pointed down the road, thumb pointed into the air, in the direction I wanted to go. There was no ticket cheaper than that for making distance and writing songs.

NINETEENTH YEAR SLOW DOWN
Lyrics and Music - RW 1971
G C G - C
I've never been real happy
G C G - C
About this my nineteenth year
C F C F
Wanted to belong but things went wrong
G C G - C
I said Lord get me out of here
F C F C
Life's a fake, one big mistake
G C G - C
Why's it so unreal?
[Ref:] G C
He said you move too fast
G C
To make anything last
Eb F G - C - G - C
So what do you expect to feel?
In my search somebody said try the church
I still didn't feel content
Everyone lied they said a prayer satisfied
But even its peace came and went
Lord what's your line? I've given you time
You give me such a bad deal
I had to keep on running
Troubles wouldn't leave me be
Things on my mind I tried to leave behind
Had to get to where I could be free
If I wanted to talk, he said you cannot walk
You've got to stop and kneel
You got to slow down be still
And know that he is God
Life's no race, let him set the pace
And things won't be so hard
For all my tears these last few years
No peace came my way
Until I listened to him
Who'll tell you everything
Just stop and let him have his say

7

Threedom Years

Lowell Tarling

The Jesus Movement is happening. Jesus has been the cover of Time magazine. There's a new type of music called Jesus Music.

Galilee launch 1978: Robert, Lowell and Genna

Three weeks into the Avondale College year, while I'm polishing the central staircase in Watson Hall, Robert Wolfgramm walks through the front door carrying two suitcases and a guitar case.

'Robert!' I exclaim, not having seen him for four years. I feel like hugging him hello, except this isn't the same eager-to-please third former who watched our high school jams. This is someone who's gone away and grown up. 'Oh hi, Lowell,' he says diffidently.

'Dave Caldwell said you've learned jazz riffs on guitar?'

'Oh,' he replies, 'a bit'.

'Well...er...' (I can see this is way too fast for him) '...let's get together after you've settled in, okay?'

'Okay.'

'What course are you doing?'

'Theology,' he replies, signalling the Assistant Dean to sign him in. I go back to my polishing.

Theology?

In time, Robert and I become proper friends. His gang and my gang become friends too. His is a younger crowd, and I like the good card players - like Adrian Miller and Arne Neirinckx - best. We play a lot of cards. Mainly a game we call Black Bitch, listed in *Hoyles Rules of Cards* as 'Black Maria'.

My crowd includes my gay roommate Dale Ratliff, a surfer called Peter Benner and two excellent Chess players, Martin Waterworth and Russell Cable. Russell plays other chess-related board games too, like Ultima and Infinite Chess on an imaginary board. He has invented his own chessboard game called 'Planar', which Martin and I don't play often, preferring straight chess or Ultima. Russell likes to read in other languages. Right now he is reading *Steps to Christ* by Ellen G White, in German. I've got a father like that.

And then, there is Diabolis, Dale's diamond python who lives in our room. It's docile. Last week there was a call for me at reception desk, 'Robbie Roy at the desk for Lowell Tarling'. I wrapped Diabolis around my waist, pulled a sweatshirt over him, then went and saw Robbie. We're engaged now and her Dad is trying to figure out what to do with her ailing maternal grandmother's furniture. There's a particularly nice grandfather's clock, which Robbie wants taken care of.

Halfway through the conversation Diabolis slid out the top of my shirt and back inside my right sleeve.

'Aah!' she screamed.

Dale, Edu and I do tricks like that all the time with Diabolis.

Robbie and I are getting married in 10 months time. We'll live next year off-campus. She'll be a high school teacher, as I would have been, had I not got myself expelled.

Dale and Anthea are also speculating on marriage, the problem being that he's gay and she must be the only person on campus who doesn't know. He talks about it all the time - *we* talk about it all the time - with Neville Dawson, as well as with Robert, Edu and heaps of other guys who aren't gay.

One evening, after I related all about my experiences at the Domain, the Yellow House and PACT Folk, Robert asks me, 'What do you play now?'

'Chess.'

'That's not what I meant...'

'Oh I see,' I laugh, 'Well, I don't play much. We had a band last year. You had one too, didn't you - at Lilydale?'

'Yeah, with Bill Smith on drums,' he shows me a photo. With Robert's hair, they look like the Jimi Hendrix Experience. 'And you? What did you do?'

'I mostly wrote the songs, especially lyrics. I spend more time writing poetry than playing guitar'.

I pull out a poem called *Vinegar* that I'm working on. I plan to send it to the church magazine *Signs*. For the past three years, the editor, Pastor Parr (Greg's Dad) pays me for my poems.

And bring me water, I want water.
Give him vinegar you sneer,
and you laugh as you lift the sponge upon that spear.

'I'll can write a tune to that', says Robert, which is unexpected because *Vinegar* doesn't scan easily. Next night, he plays a sequence of cascading notes which fits *bring me water, I want water* perfectly. Then he struggles a bit with the verse, *Watch the blood run from my side down that Roman spear...*

'Leave it with me,' he says.

Robert tells me he wrote quite a few songs in high school, like *My Nineteenth Year*, *There's A Way* and *Peter's Song*.

'Let's hear them...'

So he plays the first two meaningfully, but prances around the room for *Peter's Song* singing *Ga-dee-dah dee, Ga-dee-dah-dah* - a great babble between the chorus and the verses, which isn't a regular part of the song.

'I love that *Ga-dee-dah-dah* stuff!'

He hands me the guitar and says, 'What have you got?'

I play something I wrote called *Illegitimate Child* and a joke-song called *High Upon a Mountain With Some Beans* (written with Stewart). I think he likes the latter, he laughs in all the right places.

He asks about Robbie. They were at the same school for a time. He thinks she's 'very English'. I tell him, 'so am I'.

'Oh yeah,' he says, 'I didn't think of that'.

We talk about how he came to be at college - a guy called Peter McDougall had a lot to do with that. When he attended college Pete McDougall spent most of his time building a house in Currans Road with Terry Wilkinson. The house is across Dora Creek, walking distance away.

Then Pete McDougall kept building houses, starting businesses, making money. In Melbourne he's a big wheel in the Adventist Businessmen and Professional association.

Robert and I start swapping albums. I lend him Leonard Cohen and The Band's *Big Pink* album, and he shows up with Canned Heat and Mandrill which he explains to me and Dale is 'funk' music, which Robert likes heaps. So do we. I tell him to read *The Outsider* by Camus, he tells me to listen to *Tapestry* by Carole King. And we all remind each other that Little Richard is a Seventh-day Adventist, so there's hope yet.

Robbie's friends become our friends too, Nomi Jackson, Julene Cook, Ivy Woo. Ivy is Hawaiian, and has lots of American music not available in Australia, all of which Robert borrows from her and plays in my room. We become a bit of a 3-way club - my crowd, Robbie's crowd and Robert's slightly younger crowd.

After a while I start missing the things I did last year, my expulsion year, when I had a poetry stand at the Domain, so I start a college publication that I name *Mustard Grass*. We have a printed cover, and the publication looks quite flash until you open up to the inside mimeographed pages.

Privately, I enjoy the poetry of Allen Ginsberg, Carl Sandburg, William Wantling and Michael Dransfield. I really want to become a poet or the editor of a poetry magazine. That's what I want to do with my life. I'll support my family with the income I'll earn writing poetry.

I've got a Yamaha 250 motorbike stashed on campus behind the SHF factory. Owning a motorised vehicle is still an expellable offence at Avondale College in 1971. Robbie's parents would never forgive me getting expelled a second time so I'm crazy taking a risk like this. Maybe the fact that we don't have Dr Macdowell as principal has given me this confidence.

This college drives me nuts. 'What did you do last year?' asks ministerial student Herbie Kerston.

'I met Martin Sharp at the Yellow House!'

'So what?' he scoffs, 'I've met Billy Graham!'

Driving off-campus keeps me sane. Sometimes I drive to Newcastle at night with Robert as pillion, sometimes I go on my own. I took Robbie to Newcastle only once, she now refuses to ride pillion. She hates bikes.

> *O motor bike that I love heaps,*
> *I wish thou didn't give my girlfriend the creeps...*

Robert and I escape to see a band. Out the front, making a big display of himself is poet/presenter Adrian Rawlins. I find him intimidating. To my annoyance he's doing 'performance laughter' out the front.

'*Tully*,' I tell Robert, 'Great band. I saw them last year at the Mandala Theatre. Rawlins was their announcer and a lot better than he is tonight. He kept going on about *Tully Love.*'

The band performs, which is okay. When we get out it's 11.30 at night at night and we've nothing to do, so Robert and I decide to sleep in the streets because neither of us has ever done that before. So like a couple of hobos, Robert and I pull a few garbage bags into a shop front, and spend the night in Hunter Street. When the cops move us on, we stack another pile of garbage bags in another shop front and – apart from a shard of broken glass that cuts me in the back– we have a good three hour kip before heading back to college.

One night, while alone in Newcastle, I spot a sign, *Poetry Readings, Wednesday Nights.*

I tell Robbie, Dale and Robert about it, but they can't be bothered. So the following Wednesday I show up alone and listen to poets Terry Johnson, David Vaux read their own works followed by Ozzy Warner reading RD Laing's *Knots.*

I ask the woman on the door, 'how do you get to read here?'

'Just turn up.'

Back at the college, Robbie and I share every meal together and we usually stroll around afterwards and sit together in the library. I lend her my Maton nylon string guitar and she plays and sings a few songs, gives the guitar back and gives up. She says she hasn't got time to play guitar, she's sewing her trousseau and working out the wedding dress. Anyway, we're not short on musicians.

I often jam with Robert in the auditorium. He plays blues on the grand piano while I hammer out the chords on a borrowed electric guitar. Robert and I regularly escape college every Sunday night where we support the theology student's street mission because we get to sit with our girlfriends on the bus there and back.

The mission runs like this: a street spruiker, a student pastor with a microphone tells all the passers-by on the main street of Wyong that *there appeared a great wonder in Heaven, a woman clothed in the sun, and the moon under her feet and upon her head was a crown of twelve stars,* and nobody gives a rats.

That finishes, then Robert and I plug in our guitars and get a G-C-

D7 thing going, followed by a E-E7-A-A7-B7 rave-up called *Jesus Blues*. Suddenly there's a crowd of 40. Having built the numbers, Robert and I stop playing and the student pastor takes over again, telling them to *behold a red dragon, having seven heads and ten horns, and seven crowns upon his heads* and, of course, the people all wander off again.

So George Masters, who's running the show, tells me to stop kissing Robbie, get back on stage with Robert and get the crowd back. Masters shakes his head, 'Why should the Devil have all the good music?'

Back we go again, with Robbie waiting for me to get offstage and – it seems to me that Robert's got someone waiting for him too. *Hmm, so that's what happened between sets?*

The Jesus Movement is happening. Jesus has been the cover of *Time* magazine. There's a new type of music called Jesus Music – I like Larry Norman and Robert likes André Crouch, and we banter about *Jesus Christ Superstar* which I dislike, though I love *Godspell*, especially its staging. Robert and I we talk about this sort of stuff all the time.

'They've got a youth thing in Sydney called Salt,' says Robert, 'They want to use one of my songs. They have big combined meetings at the Ryde Civic Centre – Bryan Craig, Bev and Chris Till, Genna, Lester, Jasmine Welling, about 10 of them.'

'And that big guy – Peter Jensen,' I remember him because he completed a theology degree, changed his mind about pastoring, and is now English Master at Scots. 'I met him the other day'.

'How come?"

'He must have come up from Sydney. He was eating by himself in the cafeteria. Me and Robbie introduced ourselves and we talked to him.'

'I heard a funny story about that guy,' Robert chuckles. 'He was in the Salt committee and Pastor Craig wanted to organise a *Youth Happening*. Pastor Hill said, "You can't call it a *Happening*, it has sexual connotations, and you know what Jensen said?'

'What?'

'He said, "Well what about a Youth *Congress*, or hasn't anybody here read the *Kama Sutra*!"' That sets me off, so there we are uncontrollably laughing when Dale walks in.

We settle down a bit, so he asks, 'Why is it called Salt?'

'*Share A Little Truth.*'

Maybe Robert and I should do something together, something more sophisticated than what we play in the auditorium and on the streets.

My idea is to attend the Newcastle poets and have my poems read by someone else against Robert's guitar backing.

'Hey,' says Robert, 'You're supposed to be the extrovert, who's gonna read?'

'Robbie could, cept she won't get on the bike. Julene? Ivy?'

'You'd like a female reader?'

'Yes.'

'I've got an idea,' says Robert, who explains that because of the Peter Macdougall connection, a guy called Terry Wilkinson has been taking an interest in his progress. In fact, he lives in the Currans Road house with his wife Bev – and Bev has the clearest speaking voice. Like crystal springs.

Next Wednesday, Terry, Bev, Robert, Julene and me squeeze into Terry & Bev's orange Ford Capri. We arrive at the venue, which has the sign out the front, like I said. I say hi to the woman who said 'just turn up and read' and we tell her we're ready.

'Good.'

'Hi.'

Terry Johnson reads first,

> *Tennis in the afternoon*
> *Cups of tea at three...*

Then Ozzy Warner berates the audience for a bit.
David Vaux reads:

> *Oddly it was Newcastle that dropped the bomb...*

Then Priscilla announces me as the next reader.

I rise from my chair, tell everyone that I have written the following poems, and I sit back down.

Bev takes over, with Robert on guitar and Julene on flute. Bev reads *Ode, Vinegar, sun poem* and *stormy nonsense* and everyone is stunned.

> *yesterday i closed my eyes on the passing face*
> *of envenomed passion*
> *i dreamed i was lifted into the sky*
> *& i saw stormy nonsense*
> *& approaching faces...*

Together Robert, Julene and Bev take my words into a realm where they've never been before. Here's beautiful woman doing the reading, perfect backing for a coffee shop. I've never sounded that good in my life!

Next week I come back and read my poems without Robert and Bev, and I am just like everyone else in the room.

Well, that makes me think.

It sparks something in Robert too because we start writing more songs, and we can't stop talking about Bev's show-stopping readings.

'There's a show in that...'

Robert reckons if we can write a good script, he can build it up from the 3-piece band he's been playing with - Andrew Kingston and Rhonda Illett to something bigger. Dave Caldwell might even be interested. Robert could even score every part.

'You mean write everything on sheet music?'

I've really got to think about the meaning of this. I know Robert plays guitar, bass, tuba and piano - however writing a score for a chamber orchestra is going require skills I didn't know he had. For starters, how will he know what his orchestration will sound like if he hasn't heard it played? Composition is not like writing piano pieces and playing them back, nor is it like arrangement which is a matter of giving colour to lines that are already there. There are certain things which will produce a particular sound if done one way, but with only slight modification will sound completely different.

'I might need help from Thrifty, who runs the Music Department, but I'd like to give it a go. And a choir, Robbie can be in choir– because there'll be an angelic choir. Ag can be in the choir too.

'Who's Ag?'

'Andrea Martin,' he replies.

Robert tells Ivy Woo we're doing it.

'Who's writing the words?' she asks.

'Lowell, he's the best poet on campus,' he announces proudly.

'Lowell?' she seems taken aback, 'He hasn't even grown up yet!'

VINEGAR
Lyrics - Lowell Tarling;
Music – RW 1971

G7/6
Watch the blood run from his
C9 G/B Am9
side down that Roman spear
G7/6 C9
Must you crush me to the last
G/B Am9
though my time is near
G C G
Why is it you don't understand
F C G
The reality of what you do?
G C G
Have I wasted all my life if
F C G
these events do not reach you?
Can't you see me dying instead of mankind
Or has this excitement and hatred just made you all blind?
Why is it you don't understand
The reality of what you do?
Have I wasted all my life if these events do not reach you?
[Ref:]
Gm7sus F/G
Bring me water
C G
I want water
Gm7sus F/G C G
Give him vinegar you sneer
Bb C G
And you laugh as you lift the sponge upon that spear
Bb C G
You laugh as you lift the sponge upon that spear

L-R - Lowell Tarling, Russell Cable, Edu Neirinckx holding Diabolis (the snake), Martin Waterworth, Robert Wolfgramm

8
SALT, Thomas & Jonah

Lester Silver

A great theological debate was underway, sweeping through the pews and being preached from the pulpits. Faith vs Works. 'Father in Heaven' hit that spot.

Lester Silver

I didn't grow up in a particularly musical family. There were no instruments around and neither of my parents played or encouraged me to learn an instrument. Mum loved to sing at church and there were the Mario Lanza and Pat Boone records, but that was about it.

I remember when I first fell in love with sound. Dad had taken me to Bruce Judd's place for some reason. I must have been about thirteen, we were living in Adelaide. In his house there was a piano and while they were busy talking, I became transfixed with the beauty of sound by just banging around on the keys. It must have been pretty awful, but to me it was like a whole new world had opened up inside me. It must have only lasted a few minutes but I was hooked!

My church mate at the time was Bruce Topperwien. He was a real musician. His Dad and he used to play the trumpet or trombone and electric bass at church sometimes as a special item. Bruce offered to teach me guitar. He would come around to my place and we would have a jam session in my bedroom. I would get some Bakelite bowls out of the kitchen cupboard, turn them upside down and use them as drums to tap on with pencils while Bruce played some cool folk songs on the guitar. Somehow I got a guitar, a steel string 'el cheapo' with shocking finger numbing action. I was fourteen and I started punishing those fingertips and the ears of those around me. I started learning the chords Bruce showed me.

Dad got a promotion, Managing Director of ARTP, we were moving to Sydney. My older sister Di and her boyfriend Rob drove over to Adelaide from Sydney to pick us up. They were trainee nurses at the San. My older brother Darryl had a Simca, a black one, so he drove that and we followed Di and Rob in their Holden back to Sydney. I hung my guitar out the window and played Donovan and any other three chord folk tunes I could, all the way there.

I was never a rebel, but one afternoon a mate of mine from Normanhurst Boys High School where I going, got me to skip classes. He was a really fine musician and could play the blues, complete with harp and holder stuck around his neck just like Bob Dylan. He was short and thickset with long dark oily hair and a strong Irish accent. I could hardly understand a word he said. When he played and sang he just got lost, it was awesome. Someone with those credentials couldn't be denied.

We caught the train into the city and ended up in some music shops looking at guitars. Hung up on the walls were some of the biggest names of the instrumental acoustic guitar world, Martin, Maton, Fender, Yamaha. We were checking out all these beauties when a dodgy looking guy, who was also browsing around in the shop, randomly came up to me and asked me what I thought about the 12-stringer I was looking at. I stood my ground but didn't say much. Undeterred by my lack of communication he just came out with it, 'How would you like to own one of those?'

What did he see in me, a skinny sixteen year old kid in a grey school uniform? It must have been the hungry way I was looking at the guitars I suppose. I walked out of there with a pawn shop stub for a Yamaha 12-string acoustic guitar he just freely gave me. Fifty dollars owing to get it redeemed, expiring in two weeks' time! With money borrowed from Dad, a phone call to confirm with the shop and a trip up Oxford Street on my own, I was on my way on the train safely back to Wahroonga with my new guitar in its case. I didn't know then, but my inherent passion for music, moving to Wahroonga at that time, being 'gifted' my new guitar, and the people I was soon to meet - starting with Warren Judd who lived across the road - would set me up for an amazing five years of music and involvement in SALT, *Thomas* and *Jonah*.

Warren Judd worked at ARTP with Dad. He was a great guy and helped me tune my new guitar. My months of playing my old six stringer had paid off, I could handle the extra finger pressure required to play a 12-string. Wow, what a fantastic full sound. I played it as much as I could for hours at a time in my bedroom after school.

I had started singing along with the songs I was learning right from the beginning. Cat Stevens *Morning Has Broken* had become a favourite. A girl from Wahroonga Youth Church must have heard from someone that I played and sung a bit so she asked me to join her in a Special Item for a Sabbath Service in the big church. I was on my way.

I started getting asked to sing and play songs here and there. There were quite a few of us who were doing music at the time. Andy Vidler, Ivan and Angie Caldwell, another husband and wife couple - he used to play a tea chest bass, the Dave Hall-Kevin Were-Alvyn Backhouse trio, Bruce Judd, myself and others. The whole thing was about revival and getting young people involved and interested in expressing themselves and their faith. It was heady times.

Growing up I was totally immersed in the Seventh-day Adventist Christian world. I guess my family life was not as tough as some, but prayers and readings every evening and strict observance of the Sabbath from sunset Friday till sunset Saturday had been the norm all my life. I remember we got our first TV when I was in my final year of High School. As a 16-year old turning 17 I was too young to finish school, but the great thing about my parents was they never told me what I couldn't do when it came to the things I thought to be important - like playing music, deciding to go to the National Art School instead of Avondale College or hanging out with my not so SDA mainstream church friend Paul Bryant, who introduced me to Led Zeppelin, Black Sabbath and Norton motorbikes.

Around this time I started writing and making up my own songs. *Fussin' and a-Fightin'* was my first song and it became popular.

> *Well this fussin' and a-fightin' it goes on and on,*
> *from the day I was born to the day I move on,*
> *I'll be askin' myself, why, why, why?...*

It was a moody, angsty teenage song asking that unanswerable question - why? Bruce Judd asked me to go to Melbourne as part of a Youth Outreach Mission to sing it. On the way down somewhere near Sale, Bruce proved his Holden Monaro could do the ton. My world was definitely expanding, I was in the presence of crazy angels. *Fussin' and a-Fightin'* started me off, and when I think about it, sort of forecast the end of that path for me as well, because I looped right back into the same question when I asked myself 'why Christianity?' a few years later with the final song I ever wrote - *Aching Blue* ...

> *So much hurt in my eyes, so much aching blue in the sky,*
> *Can't anybody tell me why?*

I answered that question by abandoning Christianity.

After school I started working for Brian Stewart. He had a printing business. He knew Lowell Tarling, Genna Levitich, Ivan Caldwell, Warren and Bruce Judd and Pastor Bryan Craig who had got SALT up and running. All these guys were older than me. I had heard about Lowell. My older sisters knew about him somehow. I think it was because of stuff he had done at Avondale College. He was one of those fringe characters that I knew was a bit radical, talented, out there, in a different world than me. My mom used to whisper to me when I went to the big church in Wahroonga sometimes, 'That's Mrs Tarling, she's French' - like she was some sort of strangely acceptable outsider. The family had a reputation!

When I was seventeen I wrote a sit down musical called *Thomas* - (ie. the Doubter). By then I was playing a lot with Dave Hall. He was a very experienced musician with an awesome skillset, and he sounded just like Paul Simon from Simon and Garfunkel when he sang and played guitar. He taught me the value of repetition and practice. He was a great mentor and friend.

Thomas brought together a whole lot of my musician friends and some others I didn't know that well, like laconic electric bass player Dave McMahon who played gigs in a club over in Parramatta where people smoked and drank. He was out there in 'the world'. To my mind that made him sort of dodgy but very cool. We met for practices at ARTP. I was young and intense, I wanted everyone to know –

Oh ye of little faith, he cares for you,
Oh ye of little faith, he's gonna die for you, ooh...

We had our major one off performance at the Ryde Civic centre for a SALT event. It went well.

Not that long after *Thomas* was all over, Lowell contacted me. He asked if I would be interested in coming over to talk about writing some music for the songs he had written for a stageplay called *Jonah*.

I was a bit apprehensive, after all, there was that reputation thing and I didn't really know him. Lowell said Bob Wolfgramm was a friend of his. Wow, Bob Wolfgramm! Wolfgramm was a god! I had met him briefly when I went down to Melbourne that time with Bruce Judd. We visited his Ferntree Gully place. We went for a walk along a dirt road and hung-out on the verandah for a while. He had a wife (Ag) and a young daughter (Kelly). He was a genius musician who effortlessly got into your soul with his stuff. I had heard him play and sing a couple of times, once definitely at a SALT thing with Ivan Caldwell – these two guys were seriously good. Wolfgramm composed songs that used chord combinations and melody progressions that I had never heard before. They both sang with total feel. Hmmmm.

'Hey Lowell, where do you live? Meadowbank? OK, I'll come over.' By then I was driving and thought nothing of taking a trip across Sydney and back. We sat on the floor at Lowell and Robbie's place. He was intense, challenging, charismatic, driven and passionate, I thought he was a bit crazy. Really.

I had been working on a chord progression for a yet-to-be-written song. I tried it out on one of Lowell's song lyrics and it pretty much fitted straight away. The song *Father in Heaven* came to life. Lowell was a great writer. His ideas and words fitted together really well.

A great theological debate was underway, sweeping through the pews and being preached from the pulpits. Faith vs Works. *Father in Heaven* hit that spot. It was topical, poetic, the music was unpretentious yet moving, the words timeless, brilliant. It went right to the heart. No need for endless theological debate. *Father in Heaven* said what needed to be said and you felt what needed to be felt. It was undoubtedly the best song in the whole play. People still like it.

Lowell gave me a summary of the idea for *Jonah*, but most of the finer points went over my head. I wasn't really into plays and writing and acting. I had zilch acting experience and was quite awkward and a bit shy, but I had an instinct for leadership. Lowell offered me the lead role - Jonah. I guess the thought was if I could sing the songs well enough, then that would make up for my acting. I was young, tall and skinny with a big bushy beard, so what more did you need, right? I said 'OK'.

We rehearsed on the stage in the Wahroonga Youth Centre. We were dressed in long robes and stuff. Not many of us had any acting experience. Lowell's enthusiasm was infectious and he had mad energy. People made suggestions so we just bashed away at it and tried to get it right. Amazingly the combinations and skills of everyone involved gelled, and it came together. We played Jonah in about four or five places. It was sort of surreal. *Father in Heaven* (reprise) was the final song, *Jonah* was saved, it worked!

I fell in love with music and sound when I was banging away on that piano in Bruce Judd's house when I was about thirteen. I have been in love ever since. After I moved to Sydney I remember going to parties with my older brother and just hanging out near the stereo, drinking lemonade and listening to Oscar Peterson. My love of music had become totally entwined with my Christian faith, so when I began to question that, and started looking into other religions, it was almost inevitable that my songwriting and guitar playing days were numbered. I sometimes wonder what might have been.

My friend Paul Bryant had just started setting himself up as a recording engineer. He had suggested I put down some tracks. I had some good sounds coming out. Sort of atmospheric harmonics, soft vibes interspersed with hard struck chords and finger picking but I was getting involved in other things. My life was changing. I had met a New Zealand girl and we left Sydney to live in Auckland. I was reading *Life of a Yogi* by Paramahansa Yogananda and attending Elam Art School. I wasn't playing guitar much any more.

I was mooching around one day and saw a sitar in a pawn shop in upper Queen Street, Auckland. Ha! What was that amazing instrument? Exotic, Indian, new, all those strings, the decorations were way over the top but somehow made sense. I wonder what it sounds like?

The next part of my musical journey was just beginning.

I am still on that path.

9
Jonah, PACT Folk, Sally

Lowell Tarling

Genna liaised with youth pastors and from there the Lyceum Theatre, George Street Sydney. This impressed me enormously and lay the seeds for Galilee Records.

Robbie and I spent 1974 in Warragul Victoria, where our first child Amber was born. We often drove to Melbourne and had quite a bit to do with the Melbourne Streetpreachers. Sometimes we attended a Friday night Insight Group at Peter and Jenny McDougall's home in Ferntree Gully, which is where Robert lived with his family →Ferntree Gully.

I was writing plays now. *Threedom* had got me a commission to write a 5-Act play for the Newcastle Marionette Theatre in 1973. After that I wrote *Martin Luther* while doing my Dip Ed. Well aware of John Osborne's masterly 1961 work, I got away with it (I think) because it was billed as a 'high school' play. A final year high school student, Ken Paxinos, played the lead role.

Being a high school teacher in 1974, I started writing 'high school plays' for my English classes. The first had a Rock n Roll theme and the second was *Jonah*. These plays ran for precisely 30 minutes, because that was the length of a class period. No music, of course.

Next, my 3A class performed *Jonah* before 3B, which was successful enough to play the Assembly Hall before the whole of Sion Ladies College, Warragul. Then *Jonah* was performed in the Traralgon Civic Centre, at the 1974 inter-school eisteddfod. It received a commendation.

Then Dr E Gordon Macdowell (head of SDA Education) offered me a post at the Strathfield high school. The bugger who expelled me in 1970 offered me a post, and Robbie and I accepted!

Always, in the back of my head, I felt there was something more to be squeezed from *Jonah*. One Sunday, we visited Robert and Ag at their Ferntree Gully home. Robert and I sat on their verandah, watching their goat and discussing possibilities for the play. Sure, he *could* write the music for it. And that might have been a good idea when we were living in Victoria - but how would that work from Sydney?

Robert and I thought though a list of names of people who might do the job. Bruce Judd was a possibility - he'd written the music to a song in the *Martin Luther* play. Another was Cal Stewart - who Robert favoured. Cal had written a rather jocular piano tune to some of my words, but Cal lived no closer to Sydney than Robert. Hmm...Brian Patterson - was a hot guitarist, but he didn't write songs. Alan Thrift's daughter Karen had written a well-accepted musical - but I didn't really know her. And Ivan was a terrific singer but he didn't write songs either. Then Robbie suggested, 'Lester Silver'.

Lester had written a musical called *Thomas*. It shared the bill in 1973 at the Ryde Civic Centre with my *Martin Luther* play, which is how we met. Robert gave Lester the thumbs up, so I looked him up in Sydney. And what a find he turned out to be! Not only did Lester write all music for *Jonah*, he also played the title role. (From *Jonah* came the song *Father in Heaven*, which appeared on Sally's album.)

I had a lot of help with the Sydney production of *Jonah*. It had a cast of 16 players and three musicians, partly drawn from people who had been prominent in Salt and partly from my high school students.

Behind the scenes we had Robbie - sewing costumes. Lester - designing the poster, we had understudies and more. Ivan was musical director. The 3-piece band comprised: Ivan/vocals and guitar, Geoff Heise/bass and Dave Hall/lead guitar.

After a time it became apparent to the cast that I was not cutting it as director, so Jeannette Kemp took on that role. She brought in a choreographer – Jenny, from the Castle Hill Church. Stewart kept an eye on me. He had an acting role but, being my older cousin, he took me aside and straightened me out when I was behaving unreasonably, which happened almost every time anything came up about the church's stance on dancing or music.

Then there was Genna.

Like Peter Jensen, Genna was one of the SALT people. He had a small role in the play and two big moments. Boy did he beat them up! However, the important stuff was what he did in the backroom. *Jonah* played seven times. Someone made those bookings and I know it wasn't me. Genna liaised with Youth Pastors John Banks and Bryan Craig, and from there - the Lyceum Theatre, George Street Sydney. This impressed me enormously and (weirdly) lay the seeds for Galilee Records.

Genna's wife Anne was also involved, as understudy of all female roles. I understudied all male parts. So, I usually sat in the audience and clapped. At performances, that's all I did. John Ogg was King of Nineveh but he was sick when we played Avondale College Auditorium, so I filled in. That was the only performance that was taped and photographed, giving the impression that I was a cast member, which I never was.

Avondale was where big Pete Jensen, the heavy duty 'prophet' dressed in a black cassock, was hoisted up the 40ft high basketball scaffolding from which he boomed at the college audience beneath him and frightened the crap out of 'em.

It was also the time when - as fill-in King - I had to groan my way through *Father in Heaven* in an attitude of prayer, with Dr Clapham and other Avondale faculty members in the very front row, undoubtedly appalled at my singing. *I come on bended knee...*I made it such a dirge.

Somewhere around this time Robert took me aside and said, 'Lowell, people like you to be anarchic and silly on stage. When you're meaningful and sincere – it doesn't quite work'.

Two/three years before, I had performed with Robert on the streets of Wyong and Melbourne, with our electric guitars.

Robert - the reluctant singer, me - the crook singer.

We were on the back of a truck.

Everybody wanted *him* to sing so I'd strum up the E-E7-A-E.B7 blues-thing, set up the song.

Then he'd unexpectedly step back from the mic, give me a nod and say, '*You* sing'.

Big mistake.

Ah got the two of me walking, two of me walkin' in one man blues....

The *Jonah* production was pretty well received. Its success hung on Lester's great music and newly-found acting skills. And I got away with it because I didn't claim too much. I pitched it as high school/young people's theatre, which made it okay. It was also well received because it involved a good size cast yet very few sets.

I started wondering - maybe I was a Young People's playwright? So I read a book of simple plays written by a woman schoolteacher (whose name I forget) for the NSW Education Department. I wondered maybe I should write like that?

Throughout all this period, Robert and I would communicate, usually in long letters, sometimes on the phone. Along with Stewart, Genna, Allan, Clayton, Lester, Jeanette, Ivan and Robbie, my wife - Robert advised me on many things.

Then, quite unexpectedly after *Jonah* I was on my own creatively in 1976. Lester was becoming less and less interested in the guitar, Robert was in Melbourne, Allan was in Bermagui, I was left - as they say - like a shag on a rock. Having played the SDA circuit, *Jonah* was all over with no follow-up. In 1976 there was no 'next big thing' in my life.

All I had was my solo folk club gigs, which was PACT Folk -opening the bill for stars like Margaret Roadknight, Al Ward and John Curry as one of the three acts in the first half. Man, they didn't even know I was their support act! They didn't even *arrive* then.

But that's what I did after *Jonah*. And it got me back into songwriting.

Remembering Robert's advice, I stormed through Donovan's *Keep On Truckin*, jumped around a bit for Jody Reynolds' *Endless Sleep*, after which I played one of my own compositions, often with a slightly tedious message like, *Is That What We Are Here For?* Possibly a bit too serious...but I got away with it.

It was *Mr Bojangles* I couldn't get to work. And I couldn't see why not? I had a good solid strum, no passing chords. What was the problem?

Meanwhile Robert was living with his family in Melbourne, driving trucks, talking about studying Political Science and writing, what seemed to me, a new type of Gospel song.

Where my *Threedom* words had usually been personification, ie. *being* King Herod, *being* Procula, etc, Robert and his ragtag band of street preaching musicians would open up with, 'Have you heard the news!' (no backing). *You have been set free, oh I wanna thank you Lord - you did it for me!* Then Robert would pick up the strum. 'Once I'd lost my way...' (Colin Mack would join on mouth harp) and it was all upwards from there.

Robert's were declamatory songs.
Fully confident,
Almost arrogant.
An announcement.

Robert's song *Trinity* was a theological statement, outlining the work of God the Father, the work of the Holy Son and the Holy Spirit. Well...I didn't know you could *do* that with lyrics! A theological statement! This was nothing like the hymns Mum used to sing, like *Love Leadeth Me*. Nothing like happy-clappy praise songs. I continued sending lyrics to Robert, some of which he set to music. With Gospel lyrics I followed Robert - not the other way around.

I also wrote about a range of other subjects - Aboriginal women, living in the desert, suburban life, lung cancer, terrible radio, the A-bomb and my newborn son Joel, whereas Robert wrote exclusively

Gospel. My anti-smoking song, *Cancer* actually earned me money.

With Lester on harmonica, Geoff Heise/bass, Grahame Evans/lead Genna/coughing, and me singing/playing rhythm guitar, we recorded *Cancer* at ARTP Studios. I mailed the tape to the Health Dept and received a cheque for $120. Genna sold it to 2Double J Radio as well, and they too send me a cheque for about the same amount. I even sang it for the TV show, *A Current Affair!* As a crook singer, I was peaking.

I was playing a lot of solo spots. Also taking my guitar to school in preparation for the school concert, held each year at the Sydney Town Hall. I was on the lookout for student performers. Like, guitarist Tony Stacey, who was often booted out of class. He'd come to my staffroom and we'd jam through the rest of the period. Then there was Alison Blair and Bronwyn Bateman, a duo. And, a 15-year girl with a shock of hair and mature voice - Sally Hilder.

I'd written a slow song *Waggoner & Jones* which, coming out of my mouth, sounded like another dirge. So I gave it to Sally who sang it at the School Concert with Tony and me on guitar. There was a bigger applause than I expected, and I thought, 'Hey Sally - try another song that I can't sing...' and I gave her *Mr Bojangles*. That worked too.

Hmm...

So I asked Sally if she'd like to sing with me at PACT Folk, which had moved from Whitlam Square into a wine bar called *Journey's End* in Forbes Street Kings Cross. Although Sally was underage, her foster-Mum said it was okay.

So I hammered my way through *Keep On Truckin'*, *Cancer* and a couple more songs then announced, 'I've brought a young singer with me tonight – ladies and gentlemen, put your hands together for Sally Hilder...!' She got up and sang *Mr Bojangles* pretty well.

Next week I said, 'Do you want to do it again?'

'Sure,' Sally shrugged.

We learned the Rod Stewart song *Sailin'* as a back-up song. Now we had two. Then we added a third one. Pretty soon Sally was singing two-thirds of my set.

At school, word got around that Sally & I were performing together.

We got asked to sing at school/church functions. What we now needed was a couple of Gospel-songs...so I told Sally about Robert and taught her his *Peter's Song*. We playing it heaps, and it always went well.

But *Have You Heard the News* was our most striking song. Those call-to-action, opening lines...!

By the close of the year, we'd wrapped a 9-piece band around Sally. Sally/vocals, me/rhythm guitar, my brother-in-law Adrian Roy/harmonica & lead guitar, Martin Wilkinson/bass, Steven Wold/drums and Lianne and Michelle Wragg, Sue Boucher and Donna Golby as backing vocals. We played the school concert and sang *Father in Heaven* which everybody liked. *Have You Heard the News, Father in Heaven, Mr Bojangles, Sailin'*...fairly quickly Sally and I had a pretty solid set at church concerts and at folk clubs.

One Saturday night, at the Forbes Street wine bar, the Sally Hilder Band (Mk 1) - topped the bill and played out the night.

Sally and Lowell

10

Melbourne Streetpreachers
Robert Wolfgramm

These home 'Insight' groups - like Peter McDougall's - gave rise eventually to our own recording company, Galilee.

Streetpreachers at the launch of Sally's album, 'All My Friends Are Sinners', McDougall's house, Ferntree Gully.

In the Australian summer of 1971, Trafford Fischer, from the New South Wales country town of Wagga Wagga came down to Melbourne for an annual Bible camp in the eastern suburb of Nunawading.

One Saturday afternoon, after doing a bit of street-preaching, we thought it would be a good idea if we jumped into his FJ Holden and headed off to the Woodstock-style rock festival at Sunbury, west of Melbourne to try and save more souls. Hot on the heels of Woodstock's huge success, there were other rock festivals (such as Ourimbah NSW), but none were as spectacular as Sunbury in 1971.

As we got onto the dry dusty road, the afternoon heat was subsiding somewhat, but we soon found ourselves in the middle of a snail- paced traffic crawl with no sight of the entry gates - and his FJ did not have air-conditioning. Eventually we could hear the distant thudding and booming of the sound system. After an hour and an approaching dark, we gave it up and pulled off the road for a rest. And so I missed out on seeing Billy Thorpe and his Aztecs rocking out in a classic performance that now exists on DVD.

Streetpreaching was conducted by a disparate group of young Aussies who took to Melbourne's city streets on Sunday nights to publicly proclaim their enthusiasm for their God and the faith that united them. They were consequently nicknamed 'the Streetpreachers'. I joined them in 1970. We didn't stop the war in Vietnam or bring down the government. What we stopped was a war within ourselves. What we successfully dethroned were troubling philosophies about who we were, and why we were here. In the end, our aim was not to change the world in some grand way, but to change our individual worlds and to revitalise our church communities in the process.

So for seven years (1970-77) we, the Streetpreachers became a theatrical, public fixture in several Australian cities and country towns. Along with the Pentecostal charismatic renewal, the rise of biker John Smith's *God Squad*, and the appeal of Liberation Theology, Streetpreachers embodied the radical Christian spirit of the time and the church's belated response to the Sixties. In essence, with the Streetpreachers, the 'Jesus Revolution' with its 'Jesus freaks' - as *Time* magazine had dubbed the phenomenon in the United States – found expression in Australia.

The idea of street witnessing appealed because of its immediacy and its primitive method of eyeball-to-eyeball directness. In Sydney, it manifest in soapbox encounters in the Domain led by college and university students. In Melbourne, the Yarra Bank provided a parallel venue. But the Streetpreaching scene that evolved in Melbourne gave rise to a specific subculture that was without parallel elsewhere in the Christian church at the time. It was a time of 'phenomenal energy', as one church leader summed it, 'led by young people who didn't have maturity, but who certainly had a vision'. It was also a time of 'incredible pain' and of 'memories I'd rather forget', one of my fellow Streetpreachers later told me.

At the time, the buzz of street witnessing risked societal and official church sanctions because it was innovative and somewhat unpredictable. But it was both exciting and productive. What began in Melbourne with a specific inner city 'mission' eventually found expression in a coffee shop drop-in centre, a vegetarian restaurant (the first in Melbourne) and then a recording company (which I became involved with).

To begin with there were simply weekly gatherings of Streetpreachers at churches, then leaders, church members and converts converged for regular, informal, Bible studies conducted in homes. These home 'Insight' groups - like Peter McDougall's - gave rise eventually to our own recording company, Galilee.

In 1971, on the advice on my Academy principal, I accepted a scholarship to study theology and teaching at a Bible college near Newcastle NSW. Midway through the first semester, I joined my mates to do Streetpreaching in rural towns like Nyngan, and coastal towns like Cairns Qld and Wyong NSW.

I got involved in the Wyong street scene through the urging of my college roommate, Charlie Bobongie, a Part-Solomon-Torres Strait Islander from Mackay, Queensland. He was a singer whose style was Country-Gospel. Lowell also joined the Wyong outreach venture and we typically formed a duo to jam on the trailer stage (ie. a parked flatbed trailer) with borrowed electric guitars and making up 'Jesus blues' and 'Jesus rock' as we went along. I preferred the blues of BB King, Eric Clapton, Muddy Waters, Son House and the Rolling Stones, but we adapted our words to suit the gospel.

It was not always what other participants expected or applauded, but the leader in that Wyong venture encouraged us to keep doing it because we attracted a crowd not used to hearing *Rock of Ages* jammed as a 12-bar blues number, and they stayed on and usually applauded. Some of our jams were subsequently formalised into songs for the Melbourne street scene. When Lowell and I subsequently took to the trailer stage in Melbourne, one church leader was so displeased by what he was being subjected to, he literally 'pulled the plug' on the amplification system that drove our performance. We were angry of course, but hey, 'peace man', 'Jesus loves you', we'd say.

In Melbourne in 1973, the line-up of our Streetpreaching Jesus-Rock group varied from week to week, place to place, house to house, but on a typical night, Sam Melamed played lead guitar when he turned up or I did when he didn't. Sam was originally lead guitarist for the 60s group, the Town Criers, whose hit *Everlasting Love* was covered and re-released by U2 in the 1990s. (Sam is still doing music in Melbourne).

Colin Mack played blues harmonica, and Bill Smith was on drums. (Colin is still playing blues harmonica as a session player.) I shared lead vocals with Lowell or Debbie or whoever turned up. Debbie became a staple among Streetpreacher audiences as a popular singer. Crowd favourites included her version of *Prepare Ye The Way* and *Day By Day* – both from the hit musical, *Godspell*.

In the Sydney scene, former Rock guitarist from 60s group, *The Executives*, Brian Patterson, became associated with the Streetpreachers there.

Streetpreacher music styles weren't the only thing that worried church leaders and civic officials; we were often seen as part of the illicit drug subculture. Debbie recalled, 'The cops were everywhere, always looking out for pushers and dope addicts. They picked me up once. They thought I was pushing. They wanted to know what was in my bag because I'd been talking to this dope pusher before and they thought he might have given me something. They got my purse and went through it and said, "you've been consorting with a dope pusher"'.

The association between 'sex, drugs and Rock-n-Roll' was a stereotype still in ferment when Streetpreaching commenced. Nevertheless, the connections were real in some cases.

Streetpreachers actually converted street people who, almost without exception, had come from the Hippie subculture where this unholy trinity of personal and social vices was well-grounded. Colin was one Streetpreaching convert who typically remembered being 'out of it, tripping on acid' when he first encountered the group. For years after he continued to experience 'acid flashbacks' during Bible studies.

Greg's background included having 'experimented with cocaine, marijuana, amphetamines, LSD and mushrooms'. Vic, another hippie convert, remembered the powerful combination of marijuana and the gospel message in his initial introduction to the street preaching witnesses, 'We'd have a toke in the car before going into Adrian's Bible study'. On another occasion, he recalled the Streetpreachers spending 'a long time looking at an apple' to try and find the limits of human temptation.

By 1977, with funding from the Streetpreachers and with musical help from a number of Christian and non-Christian friends (Genna, chief among them) and professional musos (Mick Reid and Charlie Hull especially), I began with Lowell and Genna, to record an album with Gosford-based sound engineer, Paul Bryant.

Lowell named the venture *All My Friends Are Sinners*. It was released through Spotlight Records, a trailblazing non-denominational Sydney-based Christian music distributor. The album was critically well received. One secular reviewer said it set a new high in professionalism for a Christian recording produced in Australia. Songs from it made it onto several mainstream radio station playlists in Melbourne and Sydney. We were interviewed on Melbourne and ABC Rock radio (Double J as it was then). The album sold out in Christian circles and was promoted by the first Christian contemporary-music magazine, *Keystone*, and the Christian-issues magazine, *On Being*.

That encouraged Lowell and I to do two more albums of our material. In all, we used three bands: Jazz-Pop arranger Charlie Hull put one together for us, Blues guitarist Neale Farnell put another one together, and one of Australia's great session guitarists, Mick Reid, put a third band together. With these line-ups we recorded and performed and with Mick. I met and played on the same bill as Leon Patillo (ex-Santana lead singer), the late great Keith Green, singer Stevie Wright (ex-Easybeats lead singer) and American guitarist, Phil Keaggy.

Mick and Neale had a hand in the making of our third and last album, *Persecution Games*. It was a concept-protest-album developed with Lowell. Friend and Pop Artist, Martin Sharp, came up with artwork for our cover. Martin had worked with Eric Clapton (Cream's famous *Disraeli Gears* and *Wheels of Fire* album covers). He also co-wrote *Tales of Brave Ulysses* with Clapton).

Lowell agrees that *Persecution Games* was far and away the best work we produced – indeed, it got us included in the *Who's Who of Australian Rock*. Yet, as predicted by our financial manager (Genna), the album sold least well of all, as Christians were unsure of what to make of its bittersweet lyric and metal-aggro attitude. In one of Melbourne's top record stores (Gaslight), it was filed under 'Punk & Disorderly'!

As for our fellow Streetpreachers, almost all have done well in themselves and through their children.

Genna and his wife Anne run a dental design and architecture business; Elizabeth works as a book editor for a publishing company; Ray owns a printing business; Lowell is an editor and author of 28 non-fiction books; Stan and Yvonne are retired teachers and activists; Paul (died of AIDS, RIP) but owned a furnishings business in Sydney; Adrian is a successful agriculturalist in Queensland; Steve pastors a charismatic mega-church on the Gold Coast; Peter and Jenny own a mix of million-dollar businesses; Sam owns and manages a set of elite recording studios in Melbourne; Bill is a farmer on the Gippsland coast; Greg co-owns and manages dozens of karate schools across Australia; Evan owns a number of furnishing businesses in Melbourne; Shirley and Leon are property developers; Kon runs an exclusive retreat in the Daintree rainforest forest; Eric and Rhonda own newsagencies in Queensland.

Our children have become artists, teachers, scientists, lawyers, musicians, racing car drivers, ministers of religion, designers, and adventurers. Perhaps the spirit of Streetpreaching was best symbolised in Kon and Louise's eldest son, Jesse Martin, who in his yacht, 'Lionheart' set world records as the youngest person to sail solo and non-stop around the world in 1999.

SALT at Sydney's domain. Geoff Bull, preaching.
Bev & Chris Till with backup singers

HAVE YOU HEARD THE NEWS?
Lyrics and Music - RW 1973

[Ref:]
G C
Have you heard the news?
G D
You have been set free
Em C
Oh I want to thank you Lord
D G - D
You did it for me
Em Am
Once I'd lost my way
D G
Could not find the door
C Am
Locked inside myself
C D
Couldn't take it no more
Em Am
Then I found a key
D G
I had never tried
C Am
There on Calvary
C D
Where my Jesus died

When I face the judge
To pay the law's demands
I'll point to myself
Nailed in Jesus hands
Thirty-One AD
That's when I was tried
Released that very day
Out of his wounded side

Robert: If I could be said to have written a 'hit' this was it – designed specifically for Melbourne street-preaching and a staple at Peter McDougall's Bible studies. Sally Hilder did it justice with Charlie Hull and the band on Galilee's 'All My Friends Are Sinners'.

11
Playing On Galilee

Genna Levitch

Bob and Lowell were not forming a band, but a record label that was going to produce Christian Gospel music. The label was 'Galilee'.

Genna & Colin Mack

In the early 70s, I was studying at Uni. Lowell was married and teaching at Strathfield SDA High. He asked me to play a small role in a musical he had written called *Jonah*. It was fun. Lowell was great company. I knew most of the actors and singers, including my old friend PJ (Pete Jensen). Lowell put it on at several SDA venues. I asked him if he would be interested if I could organise a show at a Methodist venue.

I had made some friends (ie an interesting girl friend) in the Methodist Church a few years previously during the Jesus Movement and they were keen to see what we were doing. *Jonah* played in the Lyceum Theatre at the Wesley Centre and it was the only non-

Adventist audience to see it. On the strength of that initiative, a few years later when Bob and Lowell were talking about putting out an LP with their songs, Lowell suggested that I could be approached to be a 'producer/manager' of sorts. They wanted me to organise, book things, look after the finances, negotiate deals, market and promote the label.

The label was *Galilee*. Bob and Lowell were not forming a band, but a record label that was going to produce Christian Gospel music. 'The Gospel' being specifically Cross-centric theology. I had a vague idea what that meant and it sounded better than the Bible bashing fundamentalists I had grown up with.

The Melbourne SDA Streetpreachers were backing Bob financially. This gave us a budget. Bob was not all that interested in featuring himself on vocals, but Lowell knew an incredible 16-year-old student with a tremendous voice – Sally Hilder, she was to be the vocalist on the first album.

Paul Bryant was an Adventist who had attended my church at Thornleigh in the north of Sydney. He was a recording engineer for Jam Studio located virtually next to Gosford station, Bob knew of him. I organised the recording sessions and paid the session musicians that Bob and Paul picked to play on the first LP.

By this time I had graduated and was working in Dora Creek, a small village on the central coast not far from Gosford. Bob and his family came to stay with us in Dora Creek.

It was an exhilarating time. We were young, capable, organised, hungry to leave our mark and hoped we had the talent to pull it off. No longer constrained by tertiary educational institutions or the judgement of church elders, we were free to make it in the big world. Bob and Lowell had written clean, sweet songs with original melodies. They touched me; I fell in love with the songs, the tunes, the understated indecision, the search for love, truth and the meaning of it all. It was creative, artistic, ground breaking, heart-rending, iconoclastic and we were going to bottle it.

It gradually dawned on me how difficult this was going to be. Bob would ask me to arrange something, change his mind, and I would have to undo it. It felt capricious and irrational, but Bob assured me it was part of the creative process. Last minute flashes of decisive brilliance seem to be coupled with 'all-nighters' to meet self-imposed deadlines. This process seemed to have no overlap with my scientific world of professional calm, careful differential diagnosis, leading to a definitive treatment plan with a measurable prognosis.

I was confused and out of my depth, but immensely proud of *All My Friends are Sinners*. Bob had established his musical credentials, Lowell had extended himself in the literary/creative field and what had I done?

I had experienced firsthand the frenzy of creativity, how it arose, how it could be contained and (occasionally) directed. I saw how living in the existential moment enhanced the uncertainty, allowing options to be explored and teased out in the grey areas that could only be felt through, not reasoned. It was exhausting, I wasn't used to the lifestyle, let alone the approach.

Many years later I found myself running an architectural firm with Anne as the design director and 22 staff; those experiences with Galilee served me well. Living with and dealing with creative people has become my life and my specialty.

I was on firmer territory when I started taking the LP around to distributors. There were only a few nascent businesses (Spotlight and Rhema) who distributed Christian labels to the few Christian record and bookshops. The LP sold well. We were interviewed on Radio 2 Double J, the ABC station that went on to become Triple J. Deejay, Holger Brockman did the honours, Bob Hudson said he liked it.

I remember it was bitterly cold and windy day. The station studio was off William Street, Kings Cross, I was all hyped up and said silly things too quickly. It was up to Lowell to save the day by doing his laid-back, easy going number. I had a lot to learn.

At the end of that year Anne and I left for an extended overseas trip, which would take us through three months in the Solomon Islands then to Boston where Anne's older sister, Janice and family were living.

Going from the tropics to North America in January was a shock I was not prepared for. I couldn't adjust to the jet lag, which I had never experienced or the cold. We stayed with them for 10 days, as that is how long it took to recover.

We hit the road in a cute VW Kombi, crossed the continent on Route 66 and when we finally arrived in LA, looked for an American distributor for the LP. Bob posted a dozen LPs over and I took them around.

Distribution by Dave was the unlikely contender for our US outlet and even he was confused as to why anyone would try and *import* into the US, would we not prefer to be his representatives in Australia and allow him to *export*? He took us out to a meal in Carmelita and needed to tell us in great detail how happy he was with his newly-wed second wife. It was my first business dinner. I didn't know how to build any rapport with him so we parted on the best terms, never to hear from him again.

In our Kombi, on the way back to our camping ground, I tuned to a Christian radio station and was startled to hear a radio preacher restrict his sermon and prayers to those unfortunates in our society who were struggling in their battle with 'weight-loss issues'. It seemed to me even then, that as American religiosity has become shriller, their grasp of the sacred has become shallower.

We came back to Australia in May 1980 and to a vastly different landscape. The Melbourne Streetpreachers and other supporters had enjoyed Sally's interpretation of Bob and Lowell's songs, but they wanted to hear Bob, as they had heard him during the Streetpreaching days. So during our absence he had done just that.

Refugee was the second Galilee LP. Somehow doing the album cover production the name was changed to *BOB*. It was a tad pretentious. Peter Simmonds, a close friend, commented, 'Not even Bob Dylan has the temerity to call an album just *Bob!* Point taken. When we digitised the LP in 2013 we took the opportunity to correct the name.

Lowell had left English teaching to become a fulltime writer. Bob had quit truck-driving, fronted Uni and was completing a Political Science degree. His hard-luck days were over, Lowell's were just beginning. We had bought a 40-acre hobby farm in the Martinsville in the foothills of the Watagan Mountains. A band of friends moved to Martinsville as part of a post-Hippie movement and a nod to self-sufficiency. Anne was pregnant and all three of our daughters (Maiya, Ali and Rachel) would be born there. My first practice was in Morisset NSW.

At the end of 1980 the Adventist world was 'rent asunder' (to use a Biblical term) when Dr Des Ford was defrocked for doctrinal impurity. Anne and I had stopped going to church not long after we started dating. We both used to say, 'we grabbed a partner as we were stepping out the door'. It sounds a bit contrived now, but it was a reference to the timing, not the choice.

Bob and Lowell poured their angst, anger and dismay into the final and unapologetic album, *Persecution Games*. I listen to it now and to me, it still roars, thunders, whispers, cries, pleads, abuses, forgives and mourns the loss while acknowledging the sacrifice. It is the 14 Stations of the Cross, the Easter Passion play, the final days of Christ's life, the Plan of Redemption and Eternal Life.

It is sufficient; and it's Rock and Roll.

Robert Wolfgramm, Genna Levitch & Lowell Tarling in the studio.

12

Who is Sally Hilder?

Sally Hilder

Lowell Tarling was an English teacher who had the good fortune of having me in his class.

Sally

Some of us keep diaries and keep account of our lives. In retrospect, and particularly at this moment, I wish I were one of those people. The last diary entry I remember making was to congratulate myself on reaching the age of thirteen and farewelling childhood. Except for recording the disappointment of my brother receiving presents for his thirteenth birthday, regardless of his continuing poor behaviour according to Mum, and many threats to the contrary, I don't think I made any other entries for the remainder of the book.

Total time invested in recording a diary - thirteen days.

Well spotted - there *is* only thirteen days between me and the person I am referring to as my brother. Poor old Kevin. When I came to live with his family he immediately became the middle child by only 13 days. Including Kerrie Hilder, the family became three children all within 18 months of each other.

My name was Sally Hilder for a short period. Before being Sally Hilder I had been Sally 'three other names'. I was born the ninth child to my birth name. Fostered at six to my second name. Fostered again at 11 to my third name. And fostered again at 12 to the Hilder name. Four years of Catholicism, 12 months of Presbyterianism, and five years of Seventh-day Adventism.

During my first fostering my new parents decided it was important to make me Catholic by baptism, Holy Communion and Holy Confirmation in quick succession. Twelve months of Presbyterianism seemed to be to satisfy Welfare Dept regulations.

Five years of Adventism - a change to the day I was used to going to church, and introduction to Nutmeat, gluten steaks and Clayton's ('the drink you have when you're not having a drink') or Maison Sparkling if you were being fancy. Adventism being practised in the home also made my longing to be a member of Young Talent Time impossible - being on the show would definitely have involved me participating in secular things on the Sabbath. Could I have been a slightly bigger Minogue sister if things had been different?

My last name was legally changed to Hilder around 1977 when it seemed important to have a name to put on my driver's licence. As a result, everything official from that point on identified me as Sally Hilder. I lived as a Hilder from beginning 1974 to end of 1978 (total five years) and continued with this name until my marriage in 1988. To me my last name was never really that important. To this day I don't feel particularly connected to any of them. I don't want the name change to sound purely clinical. It was a very generous gesture by the mother who raised me for those years - four of those as a single mother. Thank you to her if she is reading.

In 1977 *All My Friends Are Sinners* was recorded under the name 'Hilder'. I've had very little contact with the Hilders since leaving their care at the end of 1978 and none for the past 30-plus years. During those 30 years I have also had very little-to-no contact with anyone from Strathfield Seventh-day Adventist High School. Being Sally Hilder in reality is just one of my lives and a long time ago at that.

The name 'Hilder' itself belongs to a man who only frequented my life for about 12-18 months. He and Margaret had only been married for a short period when I was placed into their care. Mr Hilder had converted to Adventism in order to marry Margaret. Not a good idea. He also had two sons from a previous marriage who visited for a weekend every month or so.

We lived at Warragamba in one of the old labourers' cottages, which made up the small village left over from the workers who constructed Warragamba Dam. We travelled from there to attend Strathfield SDA High for the first year or so, which involved various buses and train stations. All in all a long day.

The marriage was dysfunctional and his moods and presence were intimidating and on edge. I'm not a psychologist or psychiatrist but I'm sure there is a label for his behaviours. Within 18 months the decision was made to separate more than once and the move was eventually made to the back of an Aunt's house where we lived in a granny flat. This foster Aunt was the mother of Phil Ward.

Even though the marriage dissolved in a very short time the family continued to use the name Hilder. It is a shame that this name has been given the attention it has, considering the lack of positive input the man actually had in my early adolescence.

Landing on the doorstep of the Hilder family is itself another story. Briefly - Mr Hilder's younger brother and wife actually wanted to foster me. They lived in Camden NSW and must have had difficulty having children of their own. Their age was an issue. They were only in their mid-to-late 20s and it was considered by 'those in the department who knew better' that at 11, I was too old to be a 'natural' fit.

Margaret, I believe, was the one who suggested that a loophole could be created where they would foster me and hand me over to the others. Unfortunately, in my memory, by the end of the long process for the paperwork to be completed, the younger Hilders had received approval for the placement of two young infants. I definitely was not a 'natural fit' anymore. Poor Margaret - she made the choice to keep me in her care and found herself 18 months later as a single mother with three kids. What is destiny?

The Galilee Buildup

The Galilee experience existed for less than five years of my life. There has been recent contact, but very little over a 35-year period. Galilee time was less than living with the Hilders - less than five out of fifty years. One name period out of five....

My mid-adolescence was given to the build-up to recording *All My Friends Are Sinners* - ages 14-16. Two years. One twenty fifth of all my experiences combined. I mention these facts so that as you read you can relate a little to how hard it is to recall from so long ago. It may also help to explain the lack of political, religious, social, environmental, economic, domestic, international and cultural references expected to be a driving force in most other chapters of this book. What does a 14-16 year old think about? Everyone else was already an adult.

Lowell Tarling was an English teacher who had the good fortune of having me in his class in mid-high school (Year 9 Age 14)!

I didn't think it then but realise now that he was young. He described me in one of his books as 'the Big Girl' so I must have intimidated him in some way, because I was never BIG. Had a big presence maybe. Had big hair definitely. But so did Lowell. 'Mr Tarling' apparently used to defend me in staffroom discussions about my poor behaviour. This he would do often because it needed to be done often. He would try to convince the remaining staff that I had creative energy. It was probably due to his intervention that I was given so many considerations and reduced consequences for my 'energetic behaviour'. It also helped to be a foster child – I could always rely on a certain amount of sympathy.

My earliest memory of Lowell as a teacher was painting the back wall of our classroom – our English room. The building was brand new and we painted clouds, rainbows and flowers.

I was also the one who told him that Elvis Presley had died in August 1977. I was just reporting news – Lowell was upset by the news. Wasn't Elvis the one in the old movies that were usually screened on mid-to-late Sunday afternoon TV? *Have you spotted the developmental differences yet?*

I mustn't have been too obnoxious or hard to handle because Lowell and I ended up playing music often during lunchtimes. There were other girls as well. Think *Puberty Blues*...

The other girls (Lianne Wragg, Donna Golby, Sue Boucher, Alison Blair and Bronwyn Bateman) belonged to the pretty girl's group. It was obvious they used hair curling wands and hairspray, and wore make-up. They would have shaved their legs and gone to swimming carnivals without the t-shirt.

Now I am older, I can see that I could have been one of the pretty girls, but I didn't know it nor did I care. My hair did not mix well with curling wands and my natural inclination did not lean toward make-up or swimming carnivals without the t-shirt. I do remember their harmonies. They were like three Farrah Fawcetts who could sing great backup. It was heading into the late seventies and there were at least four young girls and a still young Lowell playing to a wine bar crowd in PACT Folk. How brave of Lowell to take it on!

There was a lot of music going on. With help from Lowell and his trusty diary obsession I can refer to playing at: Journeys End Kings Cross, the Gateway Newcastle, the Purple Door Cremorne, the Attic Hornsby...and...more.

Margaret Hilder had created a singing group about a year or so earlier. There were about 6-8 of us – *Unit of Youth* – I think. Lindy Schmidt,

Joanne Walsh, Vivien Walsh, Kerrie Hilder, Kevin Hilder, Todd Schmidt and myself. (Sorry to those I have forgotten to mention.) We sang at a large number of Adventist Churches and conducted their Sabbath School lessons mingled with a number of songs.

I can remember a significant moment for me in each program was singing:

> *Jesus what kind of man was he*
> *to die for unworthy me?*
> *It makes me want to say thank you Lord*
> *For doing what you did for me*
> *Jesus he never said a word*
> *When they spat in his face*
> *Dying he said forgive them please*
> *For they know not what they do today*

Those lyrics always impacted on the congregation, and I think that was one of the first times I realised that singing made people *feel*. Does this mean I can claim a Gospel background to my singing?

Margaret Hilder put a lot of energy into organising and transporting us all. I can remember her telling me that *she* was the one who taught me to sing. In reality, I can flashback from very early Shirley Temple moments when I would have been around five years old to around 10-11 singing *Delta Dawn* to garnish slightly more semolina for breakfast from the various children's homes (another story).

The Unit of Youth used to perform a number of role plays and dramatic presentations. Most churches received us quite well but it was a time of change, particularly with music, and there were times we were turned away from churches as we were deemed to be unsuitable. There were issues with youth, hair, jewellery and live music. One time one of our performers was escorted from the church because he role-played a homeless person and sat himself at the rear of the church. It gave us great material about 'acceptance' for the next appearance.

There was also the SOHL (Sing of His Love) Choir at Strathfield

SDA High under the care of Mr Boehm the music teacher. My memory is that SOHL was also reference to the fish that Christians used to draw to indicate where to worship and gather safely. The fish symbol was on our banner. We travelled away on a number of occasions. I never fitted into a set vocal range. I wasn't a natural alto or soprano...just loud.

In my adolescence I often found myself at the centre of debate when it came to music and dancing. There were a lot of adults who viewed both these creative expressions as provocative and sexual. The type of things that the youth of the church needed protection from. The shame was that I don't believe the youth in general perceived it the same way. It was just another way that the adults stopped the fun.

Recording All My Friends Are Sinners

I was 16... My involvement with recording was pretty much discussed between the adults. I must have been brought into the conversation and I don't remember not being willing. There is evidence that I signed a contract. It all happened very quickly from beginning to end. I've read that the concept for Galilee started in September 1977 and *All My Friends Are Sinners* was recorded in December 1977 (that's just four months).

Preparing vocally involved the gigs already performed with Lowell. Specific vocal training was one or two lessons with an extremely eccentric vocal teacher in Potts Point Sydney. She pushed my hands into her very generous body to feel the breath. She showed me how to sing in front of a candle without blowing it out. She wore bright colours with red lipstick. She told me that I should learn to sing Mezzo Soprano and that I could become the next Julie Anthony.

There was lots of adult stuff going on in the background. I was either oblivious in the moment, or I just don't remember it now, or - more probably - both. Lowell and a number of other adults were obviously discussing things with my foster Mum.

There were interviews in magazines and on radio. Luckily there were interested adults to speak on behalf of religious matters. Religion to me at that stage was - and continues to be - all about being a good person. I was never officially baptised into Adventism.

However it came about, the go-ahead to travel to Melbourne rolled around. One of my first views of Melbourne was from atop a load of boxes when Bob Wolfgramm picked me up in his delivery truck. I was to learn the songs for the album over those few days. Bob and I travelled through Victoria for close to a week making deliveries while we listened to a basic backing track for the album. Here again, I would have had no idea who the arranger Charlie Hull was.

'Oh he worked with the Daly-Wilson Big Band...!'

Who are they?

When it came to the time to record the vocals, a large group of us stayed at Dora Creek. I believe Genna had a good friend (possibly a dentist) who allowed us all to stay in his house: Lowell and Robbie, Genna and Anne, Bob and Ag, numerous small children and me. There was a room-to- room sound system, which made it perfect at the end of each day to hear the results of the session.

Each day we would travel to Jam Sound Studios in Gosford to work with Paul Bryant, the album's engineer. The experience had its moments. I had never been in a recording studio before. I don't have feelings of being overwhelmed.

My recollection is that most of the songs I recorded were put down in just a few takes except *Simon's Song* which, for some reason still unknown to me, was seen to be just not right. In those days recordings were still placed on reel-to-reel tape. Did they exaggerate or did the tape nearly break due to all the rewinding and retakes? The cry that you hear on *Simon's Song* in the final verse was real because I was feeling for both Simon and myself in that instance.

All My Friends was released on the 13 April 1978. I was still 16 and in 6th Form. I've recently discovered that about a month or so before, there had been a breach of the contract with Galilee, which resulted in me not participating in any performance or promotional work including the album launch at Peter McDougall's home in Ferntree

Gully Melbourne in May nor the Galilee Concert on 15 July at Pennant Hills Community Hall. The concert went ahead without me. There was a large line up of Christian musicians and performers with Bob Wolfgramm singing a number of the songs from the album. I'm still wondering about the reasons behind the decision to stop any further involvement on my part. Something about the songs? Something about the message? Something about hair? Something about disrespect? This decision was made on my behalf.

I do remember the record being released...not because I got to promote it, not because I performed it in concert, not because I suddenly starting receiving royalty cheques! I don't know what I was doing on the night of the launch in Melbourne or when the Galilee Concert was being presented.

My first memory of the record was when it was being held in front of me in some type of intervention organised by particular SDA relatives who wanted desperately to point out its inappropriateness - something about 'the message', something about the disco beat, something about how I didn't curl my hair enough to conceal the natural frizz, something about ungrateful teenagers, something about pretending it didn't happen, something about biting the hand that feeds you. I was 16 starting 6th Form and all that recording stuff hadn't impacted too much on my 'creative energy' at school, so life for me continued on as usual.

The completion of 6th Form at Strathfield School had its own dramas. Do yourself and Lowell a favour, and read his novel, *Taylor's Troubles*.

When I left the Hilder home I was aged seventeen and six months. I left with an almost 30-year old man, Alastair (Al) Frederick Head. That name used to sound so cool to me. One of his claims to fame was singing *Mammy Blue* some years previous and he had continued making his living playing in wine bars and performing in live club shows. He was a musician with a beautiful voice when he spoke and sang. He actually performed at Strathfield High School when I was in

Year 12. This was also organised by Lowell. There was also the possibility that we met again at a gig Al had at Ryde Civic Centre during that same year. I think that people assumed that having me connect with this man meant that I would continue to sing but when I left, I also left singing behind for a while as well. That relationship lasted for about a year.

At the end of it I was to meet a drummer Jim Buckley. Sam Melamed would add some Galilee/Melbourne connection as the guitarist, and later a bass player John Heffernan - the beginning of the second version of the *Sally Hilder Band* (1980). Lowell also had a part to play in this. It was the end of 1979 beginning 1980. *All My Friends Are Sinners* had been released for more than a year.

Early 1980 I began living with drummer Jim Buckley (another man 13 years older). We stayed together for the next three years. With varying band members, we spent our time playing a large number of pubs all around the areas of Sydney and beyond and we had long residencies at Penrith Leagues Club and the Texas Tavern in Kings Cross.

Funny how time comes around - flashback to 1979, there I was accompanying Al to his resident gig performing a Rock n Roll revival show at Penrith Leagues Club. I was nearly 18. I had travelled with him there a number of times. I wasn't permitted backstage. I used to sing along with the songs amongst the crowd and think to myself that I could have been doing that. I was thrown out one particular night for wearing 'inappropriate footwear'.

A long trip home, a young girl and a Club who didn't yet realise they were going to have me as their resident singer about 12months later (1980-81). The *Sally Hilder Band* backed a number of club acts including Georgie Fame, Little Patti, James Morrison and many others, but most of the time we headlined and filled the auditorium.

Add to this a large number of pubs, Bachelor & Spinster Balls, university graduations, weddings, private Christmas parties and corporate functions. The time was pre- Random Breath Testing (RBT) and live music was everywhere. It was bound to be short-lived as it also coincided with the formalisation of RBT and the introduction of synthesised music, which meant paying minimal musicians less money. It was very sad for drummers in particular.

We played straight Rock n Roll and for years we threw in Wolfgramm/Tarling songs – *Wish I'd Never Known, Waggoner & Jones, Two of Me Walking* and *Look a Yonder*. The beauty of these songs was that, to the audience, they just seemed to be about life and love. People related to them and would not have made any connection to Gospel.

Warren Ambrose replaced the original bass player John Heffernan, a haemophiliac who enjoyed making stained glass panels (a definite risk taker). John was a friend of Jim Buckley the drummer. John liked to play either looking at the back wall or behind the curtain. He looked a lot like Shaggy from Scooby Doo and decided when and where he felt like being social. Great guy but needless to say his time in the band was short and Warren stepped in.

This had the added benefit of introducing his brother Roger Ambrose and his friend Peter who regularly roadied for us without pay, except gaining entry into a lot of venues. They brought their girlfriends along who brought their girlfriends along who brought their boyfriends along which meant we usually had an audience.

The *Sally Hilder Band* (Mk 2) over time had a number of members coming and going. We welcomed to the line-up a new bass player Tom Sanderson, guitarist as well as Tom's friend Maxwell Macdonald Hamilton, replaced by guitarist Chris Stopforth, replaced briefly by guitarist Peter. Jim Buckley remained constant as the drummer, Tom Sanderson remained until the end on bass, as did Sam Melamed on guitar and guitar synthesiser.

During this time I was also working a fulltime job with Phil Ward of *Business Newsletters* fame. Phil was a foster cousin and in this way took me under his wing. Lucky for him I ended up being a great worker and stayed with his business for around four years. He was also a good friend of Lowell's from Avondale College days and both Lowell and I worked for Phil at the same time.

Phil's wife Nadine became like a sister to me. She and I spent a lot of time together with her daughters Maxine and Brooke. Nadine and I had both attended Strathfield SDA High together with Nadine four years ahead of me. We didn't mix together until after I finished school when I started to work for Phil. At school Nadine was a prefect. She used to recall her memories of me at school and the number of times she just shook her head at my energy and the way teachers and others would just shrug and say, 'That's Sally Hilder – what do you do!' Unfortunately we lost Nadine in July 2011, aged 54. I miss her understanding, love and late night raves. There were early times when we would travel to Bermagui where Nadine had a cabin and stay next door to Lowell and Robbie before he moved back to Sydney in the early 80s. On these visits, if we were lucky we would get to see Lowell performing in one way or another. For someone who professes to avoid singing Lowell has had his fair share of 'performances'.

Around this time I was asked to be part of the *Persecution Games* album. The whole recording experience was a little different this time around. I was still only about 19-years old but had been living out of home for a couple of years by then. The recording was in Melbourne.

The Sally Hilder Band dissolved around the end of 1982 – as did my relationship with the drummer. I began a new relationship with the third bass player Tom Sanderson. Tom and I continued for a number of years playing as a duet, with Tom on acoustic guitar. Amazing to think that we actually did dances with this format. Hard work and hard audiences.

The Sally Hilder Band:
Warren Ambrose (bass), Jim Buckley (drums), Sam Melamed (guitar) and Sally.

We are still playing with a fairly flexible band setup.

Players have included Dominic Gibson (guitar), Antonello 'Ollie' Cabitza (guitar), Tom Sanderson (bass), Chris Richter (drums/guitar/keyboard), Peter Schuhmacher (saxophone and conductor extraordinaire) Jamie Cracknell (drums), Colin McKinlay (drums), James Newmarch (drums), Steven Kleindeist (electric guitar), Chisholm Bloch (guitar), Kevin Tierney (guitar/vocals), Andrew King (keyboard), Katrina (vocals), Jo (vocals), Steven Thorneycroft (guitar), Mark Manning (guitar), Michael O'Sullivan (singer/writer/guitar), Roderick Teal (harmonica), Jules Van Dyke (vocals), Dave (trombone), and the *Gemtones Stage Band*. We have gathered together in response to bookings and provide an eclectic range of material from Blues, Jazz, Disco, Folk, and Rock.

If you were to hear us perform today this is an idea of the playlist and maybe a chance for each of you to reminisce. Music seems to continue to remain in the 70s and 80s.

Ain't No Sunshine	Leave Your Hat On – Joe Cocker
I Can't Stand the Rain	Angie Baby – Helen Reddy

When I Need Love – Leo Sayer
Fever
Rather go Blind – Etta James
Black Velvet – Alanna Miles
Young Hearts
Start Me Up – The Stones
Mustang Sally
You're So Vain – Carly Simon
Bad Habits – Billy Fields
Send Me
Chain of Fools – Aretha Franklin
Proud Mary – Tina Turner
White Wedding – Billy Idol
Shaky Ground – Renee Geyer
Hot Stuff – Donna Summer
Cold Shot – Gary Moore
Little Wing – Hendrix
Play that Funky Music – Wild Cherry
I Feel Good
Another One Bites the Dust – Queen
You Really Got Me
Master Blaster – Stevie Wonder
St James Infirmary
It's a Man's World – Renee Geyer
Long Train Running – Doobie Brothers
Cold Shot – Stevie Ray Vaughan
Difficult Woman – Renee Geyer
Rhiannon – Fleetwood Mac
Similar Features – Melissa Etheridge
Wonderful World – Louis Armstrong
Like the Way I Do – Melissa Etheridge
Fields of Gold – Eva Cassidy/Sting
Chrome Plated Heart – Melissa Etheridge
Heaven must be missing an Angel – Roger Tavares
Can't remember not lovin you – K T Oslin
Stand By You – The Pretenders
Thieves in the Temple – Renee Geyer
Sometimes Love Aint Enough – Patti Smith
New Kid in Town – Eagles
The Boxer – Simon & Garfunkel
Something to Talk About – Bonnie Raitt
Gimme One Reason – Tracy Chapman

Beast of Burden – The Stones
Thrill is Gone – B B King
Start Me Up – The Stones
Vincent – Don McLean
It's too late
Seventeen – Janis Ian
Annies Song – John Denver
Daniel – Elton John
Something
Streets of London
Grapevine
Total Control – Motels
Preacher Man
Misty Blue
Live Close By – K T Oslin
Summertime
People Get Ready
Landslide – Stevie Nicks
Cold Cold Heart – Norah Jones
Fire and Rain – James Taylor
Feeling Groovy
You're No Good
One Meatball
Walking by Myself

Crazy – Patsy Cline
In the Air Tonight – Phil Collins
Stand by Me
Wade in the Water
Moondance – Van Morrison
Bojangles
Walk on By
In the Mood for Love
Sea of Love
Girl from Ipanema
Chuck E's in Love – Ricky Lee Jones
I Feel the Earth Move – Carole King
Midnight at the Oasis – Maria Muldaur

In conclusion I'd like to acknowledge of number of people as having some form of influence in making me who I am today by being some part of who I was when I was Sally Hilder. I also know that everyone likes to see their name in print.

Huge apologies to anyone I may have missed.

Only you will know what influence you may have had – good or bad!

There are some definite names I do remember. Hello to Jo (Joanne) Walsh/Probert/Sims, Debbie Ingles, Kathy Metcalfe, Christine Peach, Sonya Burke, Kerryn Schofield, Julie and Francis Lewis, Roderick Bryan, Julie Page (dec), *Paul Bryant (dec), Debbie Smith, Ripple Nigara (great name), Carol Tew. Apologies to Jo and Barry Sims for the illegal borrowing of the old unregistered hand painted silver 1954 Austin Morris from their garage in Punchbowl!

I want to acknowledge the following staff of Strathfield SDA High who obviously had enough impact on me - good and bad - to remember part or all of their names: Mr Luchow, Ms Watson, Mr Jakes, Miss Ellis, Mr Eager, Mr Lister, Mr Veitch, Mr Hughes, Mr Wong, Mr Ho, Miss Crabtree, Mr Boehme, Miss McBryde, Mr Fiegert, Mr Bidmead, Miss Cook, Mr Sedgeman, Mr Lemke, Miss DeKlerk, Ms Williams, the staff member who cut my hair out of the fan in the locker room, and, of course Mr Tarling.

I want to thank Adventism for keeping me safe in some strange way.

To my first loves – David Hunt, Robert Harding, Peter Moller, Wayne Ferris, Stuart Moxon.

To my long lasting crushes David Gosling and Gary Munro…if you could see me now you might regret ignoring me all those years ago. If I could see you now, I might regret even mentioning a crush.

To Greg Taylor who will never admit to having a crush on me - why else did he throw things at me on a regular basis?

I have two fantastic sons both in their early twenties. The eldest Lincoln lives in Sweden as a computer programmer/app developing entrepreneur. The second son, Isaac, is on his way to becoming a Doctor of Physics. Who would have thought! They are both musically talented although they do not perform outside their circles.

I have spent over 25 years in the areas of teaching, behaviour and welfare, and I am well suited to what I do, in part by sharing different moments with each of you during the life cycle of the Sally Hilder experience.

*Not the Paul Bryant from Jam Studios.

GALILEE CONCERT
JULY 15
at 8.15 p.m.
PENNANT HILLS COMMUNITY CENTRE

Featuring:-
- ★ BOB WOLFGRAMM
- ★ LOWELL TARLING
- ★ GENNA LEVITCH

Strong Gospel Music

Northern Standard — Tuesday, July 11, 1978

STRONG GOSPEL MUSIC.
GALILEE CONCERT.
Pennant Hills Community Centre. July 15th, 8.15 p.m.

The Sydney Morning Herald, Wed, July 12, 1978

13

An Interview with Robert Wolfgramm

1980

My message is the Cross and it's a message to be meditated on and it's a very private message, Robert.

Robert performing at The Attic, Hornsby, 1980

You had some offers prior to your commitment to Galilee but you turned down several opportunities to record. What changed your mind?

Galilee didn't have the money or the structure to support me until now.

But you did turn down offers?

I haven't got much confidence in other people doing things for me, I like to do everything myself and I think that's probably why. When some people offered to record me I thought, 'All right, I've got plans to record' and they used to fire questions at me like, who's handling what? This-that and the other? They were asking about marketing, who the musos were going to be and I don't think I could ever assure them that they way I was going to do things was going to be satisfactory. Now we've set up a structure. There's Lowell to take care of whatever publicity we need. We had Genna and Paul to record it, and I suppose I built up a certain amount of confidence to be able to record it.

Sally's record gave you the confidence?

Yes, Sally's record was like a rehearsal. I guess each record will be like a rehearsal of the next one because you learn certain things each time with each mistake. And I'm not sure that I corrected all the mistakes that I made with Sally's record. I got to know the musos, I got to know who's involved, what's involved, what sort of money, who the distributors are, what the market is going to be like.

Do you think your music offers anything different from what is in the present Christian and secular scene?

Yes, for a start *I'm different* and the album sounds like me.

Is it basically a 'musical' or a 'message' LP?

It's basically a message LP. The message isn't any different really from what's in the Book. (This is a bit self-righteous, but I'll say it anyway.) I don't think that there are too many contemporary Gospel artists who are singing what's in the Book. They are definitely singing about good things, and I can't knock them for that, I'd rather listen to happiness, peace, love and joy and all the rest of that stuff. So it's good. There's a helluva lot of stuff in music as far as message goes.

Is there anyone who you feel is outstanding in contemporary Christian music?

Michael Omartian is worth mentioning. I think he's outstanding as an arranger, producer, musician and as a songwriter he's great. His message is obscure and very subtle. It's not a manifest sort of message, it's implicit in a lot of ways, and he's got his own way of writing about truth, or the Gospel, as he sees it. I really appreciate the guy for his music. He's a brilliant musician. But as far as the message goes, there's not too many guys who are really on about any dinkum message. It's always a Poppy sort of thing.

What's your message?

My message is the Cross and it's a message to be meditated on and it's a very private message. I'm singing to anybody in a particular frame of mind. I'm singing to people who are 'in the closet' rather than 'at the party'. I don't think my music is performance music. I think it's more a meditative sort of music.

On what basis do you say that?

For one – it's very serious and I think that comes across. *Refugee* is a serious album.

What about Born to Die? That's a boppy sort of track.

Yes, but I think the message overpowers the music. On the album there's all these different styles of music – there's the Caribbean stuff, there's Country – but even so, the message is so serious that it crushes out wanting to get up and dance to my music. Listen to Keith Green – his music makes you want to get up and celebrate. I think my music is more like James, 'Be miserable and mourn'. It's not celebratory music. It's not music for celebrating anything other than the fact that it's music designed to make the listener sit down and listen to some songs.

Your message is the Cross – well, what about it?

I think the Cross exists at quite a high level of abstraction. It does for me. In other words it doesn't intrude into everything that I am, all the time. So in a sense the Cross is in a compartment. (Sanctificationists are going to hate this but anyway, it's a fact.) It's in that compartment in a box called *Philosophy* or *Ideology* or *My Personal Belief About Religion*. So it exists at a fairly high level of abstraction in a realm called *Bob Wolfgramm's Personal Philosophy*. I am not JUST a religious person, I'm also a social person, I have political views and views about a whole stream of things. So in that sense it is very compartmentalised. It exists 'up there', in that religious side of me. I see the Cross as the answer to what we call the Sin Problem.

You don't believe in the Social Gospel?

I don't believe that what call the Social Gospel necessarily has anything to do with the Cross. I believe that I can believe in the Cross and at the same time be a Socialist-Marxist and push for humanitarian reform and social reform and push for a social gospel. But I don't believe that's tied to the Cross. If it were then what about many other people who push for social reform? They don't all base their practical programs and ideologies for social reform on the Cross. They base it on some other philosophical notion. I'm saying, 'Sure, I do strongly believe...(if anything I'm more Marxist than I am Liberal)...' but I don't believe that it's got anything to do with the Cross. I think people who push social legislation because they say it springs from the social implications of the gospel are on the wrong tram.

I saw you perform and you said, 'I'm not into talking in tongues, I'm not into Radical Discipleship, I'm not into Liberation Theology, I'm into the Cross'.

That's right.

Why haven't you attempted to fuse the Cross with a social message?

Because the Cross is above that. It's at a higher level than that. I believe that the Cross only serves to remedy a personal situation. It is the most personal message. It is the deepest spiritual message and it only confronts you at a personal level. Because it's so personal, I don't believe you can extrapolate from the liberation of the Cross. I don't believe you can extrapolate from the fact you've now found joy, happiness and peace. I don't think that you should feel that 'because it's the answer to my personal situation' I don't think you should give it as the answer for everybody else. I don't believe in what we'd call *evangelism*.

You are anti-evangelism?

Yes, anti-evangelism, anti-Radical Discipleship, anti- all of that.

You're not just saying you're not into it? You are saying you are <u>against</u> it?

I am against it because they premise their social action on the Gospel. I don't believe the Gospel demands you do that. I believe all these things, like social reform, can spring from any philosophy of life. You have got social reformers of every hue and colour, and what I am against is the institutionalising of one's philosophy and saying, 'Ahh, the Cross means I will be a *better* social gospeller than anybody else'. That's just crap. Now, I believe we should be social reformers, not because we believe in the Cross but for other reasons that spring from the outside - like the way society is structured, notions of social injustice - secular reasons. It's nice. I think it's really neat saying, 'Because I've been treated this way in the Gospel, therefore I ought to forgive everybody else'. That's all nice, and I accept all that. But I don't believe that ought to be the motivating factor for doing social good works.

What ought to be the motive? Social decency?

Yes.

Mankind's moral code should be enough to make people love their neighbour? God's love is like an extra blessing?

Yes.

You are canning the idea that 'because God has forgiven me, I should forgive everybody else', yet these words are literally taken from the Lord's Prayer?

That's all right. 'Do unto others as you would have them do unto you' is the Golden Rule (or whatever). But it's not predicated on a God-human relationship, it is simply 'do unto others as you would have them do unto you'. It is a primary source, but a secondary source is a religious one. What God has done is a bonus reason, an added reason why Christians ought to be humane and believe in social reform. The primary reason is just a sense of human decency, that's all.

I want to jump back to what you said about anti-evangelism. This seems strange coming from someone so deeply involved in the Melbourne group of Streetpreachers?

Perhaps I didn't make my terms clear. If evangelism means a special kind of project where people have to be reached, I'm against it because it doesn't conform to the New Testament concept of evangelism. The Apostle Paul, when he preached, he didn't spend time devising strategies and tactics, using vast amounts of money to reach the people. He just taught and preached to whoever was listening. Also his audience was Jews of the Diaspora and they were all familiar with the Old Testament. He also had Gentiles. There were no gimmicks, just the simple message of the Cross. Nobody today gets up and just preaches the Cross.

But your songs 'Good Samaritan' and 'Refugee' are about social concerns?

If you notice in both those tracks, I haven't tried to tie down and say, 'Refugees deserve our help because we are Christians'. I believe they are people in need and that if you are a normal human being you ought to see that need and relate to it. I don't believe that the fact that we ought to give them help has anything to do with our Christianity. Being a Christian does not make me want to be a Good Samaritan to anybody, I want to be a Good Samaritan because they are a person like me and if we swapped places that's how I'd want my fellow human being - regardless of whether he or she is a Buddhist, Baptist or whatever – I'd want that person to help me.

What is the song Refugee about?

It is about refugees. Some people will tell you refugees have always been the upper-middle class elite in any society who, when they're taken over by another power group or another elite, are simply the Haves fleeing their country, seeking refuge in another country where they can become upper middle class once again and thus maintain their status, position and everything else. There are some Marxists who haven't got very much time for refugees because of that. They see it as a class thing. But as far as I am concerned a refugee is anybody who needs help.

You once said the song was about Jesus - after the Cross - presenting himself to the Father...?

I think he too was a refugee, there's no doubt about that. I think he was a refugee while he was here on earth and he said so. No place to sleep, no place to stay, all you others have got your homes and things. So it is about Christ. He is the refugee, and so am I, so are the people from Vietnam and Malaysia and wherever else they come from - I don't care, I think it's immaterial. If somebody comes knocking on my door and says, 'Here I am, I need help' I wouldn't help 'because I'm a Christian', I'd help because I'm a person like him or her, and I think that ought to be the basis of any social action. That's where I strike trouble with the Liberationists who are always berating Christians for not living up to the message of Jesus Christ. I believe that if you are just a person - that ought to be the grounds for helping somebody else.

Has being black affected your political views?

I have to say yes.

Do you feel black?

I definitely feel black. When I was a kid growing up I'd only feel it when there was an explicit demonstration of racism. Other than that, I used to think I was just one of the kids. When someone would say 'Oh, you're black' then it would be made aware to me that I was different. Now I feel different all the time.

What makes you feel that way?

A couple of things. But let me tell you this first. When I was in Matric I studied Australian History, and when we did Australian history we got into the Aboriginals. I looked at it through Whiteman's eyes. But now a few things have happened to me in life, maybe I'm just getting older, but I'm doing Australian Political History in my studies and it's as if I'm living in a different country. History, when you are a kid, is just so Whitewashed, so biased. Re-doing it now at a tertiary level it's just unbelievable. It's made me feel like an alien, it's very unsettling. I was naïve - put it that way. But right now, I see myself as black. I identify with black problems here in Australia and overseas and now - yeah - I see myself as a black person in a White Australian society.

How about you - yourself? Are you a musician? Producer? Political scientist? Songwriter? Or are you just Dad?

I am not a musician predominantly. If I were, I'd be seeking a musical career, I'd be pursuing a life exploiting my musical abilities, talents and all of that. Music for me is a very personal thing. The songs I write are personal songs, reflections about the Cross. So music and religion is very much a sideline. I believe first of all that I am a person - a secular person - before I am a Christian. The music, which is tied to religion, tied to the Christian side of me, takes second place.

Why did you record, if you're not seeking a musical career?

It's a hobby.

What would you do if the record was a hit?

I'd resist it.

What do you hope to accomplish as a political scientist? Are you staying in Australia or returning to Fiji?

I want to go back to Fiji.

A political correspondent?

Probably, I want to get into that side of it. I believe primarily that the problems that face us are political problems - by 'us', I mean humanity - I don't believe that Christianity ought to intrude into politics at all. In fact, whenever it has it's stuffed it up for everybody else who isn't a Christian. I believe basically that if you keep your religion out of it you'll be all right. I don't believe that Christianity has any place in politics nor do I believe that politics is a purely practical kind of thing whereby people can organise society and is contingent upon beliefs in justice, equality and things like that. So yes, I guess I see myself more as a political animal than anything else – musician, songwriter, or...?

Performer?

Definitely not a performer.

Does that explain the discrepancies between your performances?

I'm moody, I guess. I'm a big believer in spontaneity. I can't practice, rehearse and organise structured performances. I'm not into an 'act' and all those sorts of things.

You did have a band? You played pubs and did all right?

Yes, that was all right. It's easier to hide in a band. By myself it really depends on the situation, what the crowd is like. I'm really not a worker in that respect. I'll work hard at other things. I enjoy getting into debate on some political point. But music – which is as much of a challenge – I don't like working hard for people to enjoy and I don't even conceive of music in terms of work. And if you're going to be a performer you have to.

If you're not interested in a musical career, why did you make the record?

I made the record because friends wanted to hear what I had to say about the Cross, that's why.

Why did you get involved in Sally's record?

I got involved in Sally's record because I was debating which way to go. Seriously, at that time thought music might be a life for me. I saw then that it's really a hobby. I'd go as far as to say if you confronted me to do another album today I'd say 'no way'.

How to you feel about Sally's record now?

Most of them I still like, but I think Sally should get into the singing-thing because she could make a fist of it. But for me, I don't know, I really have a lower opinion of the music scene now than I had before. If you asked me to do another album I'd say 'it's not worth it'.

But you'd be keen to record other people?

Oh yes, because it's a good hobby, like some people enjoy playing golf or go swimming. As a sideline I'd really love to record every Tom, Dick and Harry just for the fun of it. I'd be dropping in on everyone and putting together an archive of street music.

You have a few critics. Would you like to comment on the youth minister who described you as a 'self-righteous prophet who specialises only in negativism'?

I probably am (laughs). That's my only comment.

And the one who said you are 'pig-headed' and 'difficult to get on with'?

That's probably right too, you can't disagree with what you are can you? (laughs) If they say that I'm like that, then I'm like that to them. This is a very phenomenological view (laughs). If I have been lousy to someone or criticized them, well...they right in saying that. Some people seem to think that in the Christian music business everybody have to be 'nice', but they don't understand that there's nothing that exempts Christian music from any other philosophy. They are pushing a philosophy that I have as much right to disagree with as anybody else – Sid Vicious, Elvis Costello, or whoever. If I disagree with someone's point of view, I tell them. And with most Christian music, I disagree with it. So I tell them, 'Look, I don't like that kind of music because it's based on all sorts of non-Biblical, experiential, subjective, romantic notions of what Christianity *ought* to be'. Most of that stuff is non-scriptural. For all their goings-on about calling it *Gospel* music and 'this is the sort of thing that happens to you when you become a Christian' – it's garbage. Why should I be nice to them just because they are 'fellow Christians'. If all Christians had to be 'nice' to each other, where would you get? What about self-criticism? It's the best and most constructive thing in every human endeavour. It's good to be self-critical and it's good to knock all the time, provided it's for good rational reasons. And if you can supply good reasons why something ought to be knocked, then it ought to be knocked. If I knock Nazism and the carryings-on of the National Front, I don't knock it because they hate Blacks, I knock it because I see their behaviour as threatening the human fabric, destructive to human happiness.

Why do you make these criticisms of so-called 'Gospel' artists?

Because they're not based on any sound scripture. If I had the words here I'd read them out, I would say 'show me where that kind of sentiment is expressed in scripture? I guarantee you can't find it!' So I challenge them. I say, 'Show me where your music is *Gospel* music?' Firstly, you have to define what the Gospel is, and they're going to try and tell me that the Gospel has got to do with good feelings, good tidings about how Jesus has come to dwell in my life and 'now I'm trying to live like him...'. I'll show you in scripture that it's not 'Jesus in me' at all. I'll show you in about 50 different places in scripture where it's about the Cross, what Jesus did on the cross and that he died for our sins. I can show them and say 'there you are!' When we do Christian music we must remember that we are pushing a point of view, and the point of view that we are pushing has to stand up to scrutiny. If we say that we are representing Jesus Christ to the world, we have to compare it to what it says in the Book. That's where we find out where Christianity is – in the book called the Bible, right? And if I say 'I am a Gospel singer, I am singing a *Gospel* song'. I listen to the words of their song and say 'I think you're a liar because show me in the Book where Jesus Christ said anything like what you've just said? Show me where he defined his terms the way you do it?' It is popularised, counterfeit, deceitful, misrepresentation of the worst kind. Seriously. I mean, if somebody got up and said 'I represent Sally Hilder, I'm going to sing you a song about Sally Hilder...' and the guy sings all about himself not Sally, I'd say, 'you are misrepresenting her'. These guys come along and say something 'nice' about Jesus. They use his name in it. They sing about how happy they feel, how they've had ecstatic experiences about it and I say, 'show me in scripture where that is supposed to be your message. Show me where the disciples represented Jesus like that?' If those guys could back up what they are saying I'd be happy, but I know they can't, *you* know they can't and they know they can't. Is that negativism at its worst? They'll probably all write me off now and say 'he's not a nice chap, that Bob Wolfgramm, he's not compassionate and understanding'. I say that's all right too because neither was Jesus to all the religious counterfeits of the day and neither was the apostle Paul. He didn't worry about telling blokes off about misrepresenting Christ. Most of the Pauline Letters were written to counteract the counterfeit. I feel that popular Gospel music is misrepresenting Christ.

You feel it's misrepresenting Christ by being what?

Not only by being subjective, they're also saying things about Christ that are irrelevant.

Such as?

Such as 'I was lost, he found me, and he made me feel fantastic'. They are pushing a Christ who is full of wonderful things and niceties - a candy-coated Christ. They make everything swing on the visibility of their Christian experience. I am against that.

One last question - what is 'Thomas' Song' about? Is there an element of your personal negativism in the song?

Probably, but it also reflects the fact that if you look at the Cross through human eyes and try to understand what it is about, you can't do it. But if you view the Cross through God's definition of it, you have to accept that it is good news, your salvation event. *Thomas' Song* looks at the Cross through unenlightened eyes.

14

Persecution Games Recording Sessions 1978-83

Robert Wolfgramm

> *It was that small mutual tick to that version of Fighting Man that triggered rehearsals in 1980 for what became Persecution Games' dark/experience side.*

Here we are in the alley beside the studio on the night of our recording. Greg (second left), Doug (rear, third left), John (rear centre), Neale (crouching third right), Phil (second right), and Colin (right).

I can't recall whose idea it was that led to *Persecution Games*, but my desire to complete a trilogy was strong. Lowell and I had many new and old songs left on the shelf after *All My Friends Are Sinners* and *Bob/Refugee*. And having released those two albums within a year, I was high on confidence and sure that these other songs would benefit from treatments by a wider circle of musical mates than we had hitherto used.

Work on PG started almost by default in 1978. I had begun playing and singing with Greg Hughson's band rehearsing in a room in

Heidelberg (in inner north-east Melbourne) that is now used, coincidentally, by my son Dylan's employer. Greg and fellow streetpreacher Colin Mack had found a bass player, Doug, and they were auditioning drummers and lead guitarists when I joined them. My interest was to use the band to promote the just-out Galilee albums as well as to contribute to whatever projects Greg and Colin had in mind. They understood that and were keen to help me out having themselves been key performers in Streetpreaching (over the previous five years) as well financial supporters of the Galilee albums.

The Heidelberg rehearsals were hilarious as they were adventurous. No sooner had Greg, Colin and Doug lined up a performance for the still forming and unnamed lineup, we were immediately put under pressure to find a suitable drummer and guitarist. On Sunday 20 August and the following Sunday, we rehearsed all day. A parade of drummers and would-be lead guitarists would file upstairs into the room, set up, play the 12-bar blues jam we prepared - as well as one or two of my songs - as best they could, after which we would show them the door and tell them we'd be in touch.

The first successful lineup to result from this familiar and tedious exercise were the additions of a guitarist named Doddy (hailing originally from New Zealand) and a drummer named Des (who was pop singer, Colleen Hewitt's brother). Doug the bassist had a 4-track reel-to-reel and taped our rehearsals. I still listen to my cassette version. I love Doddy's ethereal guitar sound – always floating out there above the song. Des's drumming wasn't pretty but it was forceful. I'm not sure how many gigs we played, but Monash Clayton was one and a pub in inner Melbourne was another.

For whatever reason, another drummer and guitarist were needed for a later set of gigs and we settled on new drummer Phil, and Neale Farnell, a young, hard-drinking, teenage bogan whose lead guitar work simply stunned us. When he left after his audition, we jumped about laughing at our discovery - God was to be thanked for bringing him to us! That lineup was settled for the next set of rehearsals when it was decided we needed a keyboard player. In walked John, a little older than us. He was English with a Ray Charles R'n'B style and a cheerful jokey manner that complemented the personality balance of the band. Our first band name was *Passport*.

With this lineup, now re-named *Southern Lights*, we shifted rehearsals to drummer Phil's house in Hawthorn and then did a couple more gigs. It was then decided we should try and record with this lineup – a few of Greg and Colin's songs and a few of mine. John had a couple of songs as well. If I recall, even Doug threw one into the mix. The overall intention was to have something on cassette that the band could hawk around to get work.

This is the 1978 *Southern Lights* lineup that headed into BB Rolls's studio in Collingwood one night for an all-night discount rate session:

The recording wasn't entirely good – the sound on the tape didn't match the energy of the performance, but the mood was great. I had just finished a three-hour political philosophy exam at Monash (Caulfield) and being my last exam for the semester, I was up for anything. I don't know who took the photo, but I was quite merry. Here is another photo of that occasion...

Neale in the studio laying down his guitar lines

Nothing came of the recording as far as I know and I do not have a copy of it, but the Saturday after I was scheduled to perform at our first and only *Galilee Concert* in Pennant Hills Civic Centre in Sydney. It was premature and too costly to think of taking the newly formed band up, so I soldiered up alone and with a vicious flu. Joining me on stage for that gig was Sam Melamed and Colin Mack.

Early the next year (1979) I performed at Ku-ring-gai College (on Sydney's North Shore) with a band Mick Reid put together featuring the cream of Sydney session players such as Peter on keyboards, Graham on bass, and a drummer from the Channel Nine showband (which played Midday With Mike Walsh mostly).

Then in December 1979, I got to play the *Newsong Christian Music Festival* – the first of its kind – at Brookvale Oval, Sydney. Some great artists appeared there. Keith Green and Leon Patillo among them. Mick put together the Ku-ring-gai College lineup again for me except with a new drummer, Greg. We went over well.

The thing is, during that year I had also begun assembling some new songs – at first alone and then with a few from John Ballis - for a concept album I tentatively called *Barabbas*. Sometime in late 1979 I was ready to record a couple of these songs with my Melbourne band mates. Greg, Doug, John, Neale, Phil, Colin and me (see photo) is the *Southern Lights* lineup that headed into BB Roll's studio in Collingwood one night for an all-night discount rate session. We headed into Crystal Studios to do a demo version of *Fighting Man* with words by Lowell. I sent the cassette copy to Lowell who liked it. I've still got the originals.

But it was that small mutual tick to that version of *Fighting Man* that actually triggered rehearsals in 1980 for what became Persecution Games' dark/experience side. And alternately, the gigs I had done in Sydney with Mick and the band were to become the foundation for what was Persecution Games' light/innocent side.

At a studio in Chapel Street, South Yarra, I rehearsed songs, with Southern Lights, Greg and Neale taking charge of arrangements, but with the band that now comprised Con and Chris interchanging on bass, and Lee on drums and calling itself *Straight Liners*.

In 1981 we started recording at Mixmaster Studios in Glenhuntly with Rik Vander Veldt. A year later we were still recording there and it was called Tiki - Rik, having bought out the studio. As was standard, we laid down the backing band tracks then bounced them down from eight tracks to four tracks to allow vocals and overdubs.

At the end of 1981, beginning of 1982, Sally turned up for her share of vocals for the project. It was a hoot. Rik liked the songs, he set the studio up nicely for us and helped us get the sound on tape. Meanwhile, Sally and Neale got along like a house on fire. I was a bit jealous and the tension undoubtedly helped create some of the energy that drives the dark side of the album. We did the crowd overdubs as well as record the album's 'quartet' (from Lilydale Academy staff).

Then the project lapsed for a year until we could get more money for the project, and Mick and the Sydney band organised for their sessions. These were done at Northsound Studio at Berowra, north of Hornsby. John Keech and Les Marton were in charge of the desk there.

Where the Melbourne sessions were rough fun, the Sydney sessions were professional and composed. Slick. I had played the songs through to Mick who had already played them through with the brilliant lineup he'd assembled for us - Greg Henson on drums, Greg Lyon on bass, Sam McNally on keyboards, Alison MacCallum and Janice Slater on backing vocals, Michel on pedal steel, Mike Kerin on fiddle, and Mick himself on lead guitar. I also got the children's overdubs done there, thanks to Ivan Caldwell's contacts.

We mixed the entire album down with further overdubs at Riversound Studio in Riverwood, Sydney. The great KO Kazokas was on the board with occasional help from Paul Bryant and myself. We also got overdubs of the 'Trio' parts (Mick, Mike, and myself) and more 'crowd' overdubs with Ivan, Sally and Lowell there.

The most memorable *Persecution Games* overdubs came with Neale who was needed to strengthen the guitar parts on a couple of the Melbourne-recorded tracks. He and I flew up to Sydney early in the morning of the booked session and went straight into the studio. It was about 11am and too early for Neale to get into the mood of the track (*False Witness*) and he asked for a slab. We got him that and within an hour we had him at his best - firing fuzz into the song's long fadeout break. KO miked his guitar amp close and then put another mike at the other end of the studio for reverb effect and it worked a treat. With the job done, it was back to our motel room at Kings Cross before our early morning flight back to Melbourne. I saw some sleep, but Neale sat up most of the night watching cartoons.

After the album was mixed, it was left to my colleagues to get the cover and inner sleeve artwork done and get it out. And that is their story.

15

Persecution Revolution, 1980-1982

Lowell Tarling

Persecution Games was moving into virgin territory. I can't imagine Gospel music going where we went next.

There was optimism in the 70s that died within us before the decade was through.

In 1975 the Methodist Church charged the Rev Ted Noffs with heresy. This is the guy who ran the Wayside Chapel, the only Christian Church with street-cred in Sydney. I was a regular in his Upper Room and Wayside Theatre between 1968-1971, especially 1970. I bumped into all sorts there, several ex-Adventists from school, like Halcyon Fraser and Harold Macfarlane who wanted to be a hermit.

Why we should slide doesn't make sense theologically. The Jesus People of the 70s were actually longhaired Fundamentalists. The Radical Christian Front – ie., those who questioned the Immaculate Conception, the Divinity of Christ, etc, were not us. We were all about the Atonement, and Rev Fred Nile actually declared, 'I find no evidence whatsoever in the teaching of Jesus for any single doctrine of the atonement.' Yet we/I absolutely supported him because of his practical Christianity.

December 1979: the Catholic Church stripped Hans Kung of his license to teach as a Roman Catholic theologian as retribution for rejecting the doctrine of Papal infallibility. This was duly noted by our crowd.

September 1980: the Seventh-day Adventist Church stripped Des Ford of his license to teach as a SDA theologian - as retribution for *what?* Preaching the Gospel - that's what!

Now, I felt like a real idiot for losing my natural mistrust of religion for almost a decade.

With a third album in the pipeline, Galilee Records had been set up specifically to voice that very Gospel. Sacking Ford spared us from repeating ourselves, resulting in the most unusual Christian album ever made.

Meanwhile, Genna was a practicing dentist. He and Anne enjoyed travelling. He'd practiced in Trinidad and other places, simply to enjoy local culture, and they came back and told us all about it. In 1980-82, their main focus was a Medical Centre, designed by Peter Simmonds and managed by Genna in Morisset NSW.

Having completed his undergraduate degree in Political Science, Robert was now working on his MA thesis and reading Sociology at Monash University, Melbourne. Although he never broke with the Seventh-day Adventist Church, in 1980 he was freewheeling, freethinking, and attracted to Universalism.

For my part, I left teaching under a cloud, having been accused of 'insubordination' by the School Council. Sally (completing 6th Form at the time) witnessed the whole incident.

In 1979 our little family moved to Bermagui NSW where I became a lake fisherman because that's what my friends Allan Broadhurst and Clayton Simms did for a living.

I was a terrible fisherman - poor and very pissed off with the world. Even the Gospel had let me down. The day Robbie and I heard of Des Ford's sacking was the day we officially resigned from the SDA Church. Robbie was attracted to Hippie handmade homes culture. I was attracted to Antinomianism. Plus, I was furious. Furious that, after being against the system in the 60s, I'd devoted my 70s to fiddling with its nipple! I had a BA Dip Ed plus five years teaching under my belt, yet now - I was barely able to feed my family and living in a poorly constructed hut that leaked and one night a possum came in.

That was my Damascus Road experience, I suppose. Clayton used to always say, 'The trouble with you Lowell, is that you've never worked with *the men*'. Now, here I was hauling fish on Wallaga Lake, catching very little and wondering what former-teaching compatriots Julene Cook and Lester Lemke were doing right now?

Yeah, I vomited at sea when working on a shark boat. Yeah, I got sacked from the shark boat and replaced by a big strong woman. There was 12 months of this humiliating stuff, and then – salvation! - I got a Literature Grant. Along with being published by Penguin, it gave me confidence to declare myself a 'writer'. But - as I said - there was 12-18 months of this lake fishing stuff – Mullet, Leatherjacket, Trevally, Blackfish (Luderick), Bream, Flounder, Flathead, Blue Swimmer crabs - and one great day a 6 kilo Jewfish (Mulloway)!

> *Look at me Jesus, I'm a fisherman*
> *Pulling my nets with a cold cold hand*
> *The wind comes up and the seas are rough*
> *Lord you know these times are tough*
> *The ruling class gets on, the ruling class gets on*

I was a weird fisherman I guess, because I was always reading while on-the-job. I recall finishing off Herman Melville's *Billy Budd* by torchlight under the Wallaga Lake Bridge while waiting for the poddy mullet to hit the net. More significantly, Wm Blake's *Songs of Innocence* and *Songs of Experience* seemed to encapsulate my shift from youthful optimism, when I believed in stuff, to the cynicism I should have never have lost.

With Robert in one ear, telling me about political science and sociology, and watching everything I once believed in turn to shit, I really enjoyed reading *The Anarchists* by Roderick Kenward.

Then, I got to ruminating about Robert's truck driving mid-70s. That must have been pretty tough too…driving to Griffiths and all those country towns, with his wife Ag and two little daughters, Kelly and Talei at home.

> *Look at me Jesus I'm a trucking man*
> *Driving my load all across the land*
> *I sleep the nights all alone*
> *Lord won't you care for my kids back home*
> *The ruling class gets on, the ruling class gets on*

Meanwhile, Robbie was doing hard slog too. In 1980, everything was hard. We were *all* cutting our teeth on something. Robbie was designing the first stage of the house we later called *Apocalypse Cottage* and she was physically digging holes and moving earth. This is a builder's verse but the builder is a woman, which is why we got Sally to sing Robbie's verse:

> *Look at me Jesus, I'm shifting sand*
> *Sweating in the body, I've got a blistered hand*
> *I've been lifting logs, carrying stone*
> *Trying to build my kids a home*
> *The ruling class gets on, the ruling class gets on*

I first heard Robert's *Save Your Grace* sitting with Robbie and the Wolfgramm family in the audience, at the 1978 Galilee Concert in the Pennant Hills Community Hall. It knocked me out, like the first time Robert played me *Have Your Heard the News*, *Refugee*, *King of the Ghettoes* and other 'major' songs. *Save Your Grace* became the Gospel centrepiece on the *Persecution Games* album.

> *Save your grace. I'm just a waste*
> *Don't pick me for eternity*
> *Save your pearls, for the rest of the world*
> *I'll spend my time, drinking wine*

...and five years later, when *Persecution Games* was actually released, I was indeed spending more and more time drinking wine.

Side A: After passing through nostalgic sentimental church music -*Just As I Am* and *Jesus Keep Me Near The Cross*, the optimism of *Just a Boy* and the anticipation of Muslim religious influence in *I'm A Tryer*, the mostly positive sentiments of Side A's *Songs of Innocence* draw to a close.

I call this the Telecaster Side, because that's what I imagine (Robert's collaborator on all three Galilee albums) guitarist Mick Reid was playing. Mick, the guitarist mainstay of the Slim Dusty Band for years, has described Robert as 'the second best songwriter in Australia - after Joy McKean'.

'Good one Dad', mocked Zoë, 'Side A and Side B - *in the CD era!*'

I call Side B the Stratocaster Side, because that's what I imagine Robert's collaborator on Side B, guitarist Neale Farnell was playing.

Side B: the listener is assaulted by the bite of Neale Farnell's driving guitar and the band is swayed by Neale's banal moral influence, which injects Side B's *Songs of Experience* with ungodly rage for tracks 2-4. The album closes with sadness – despair at our lost innocence.

What was that song by The Who?

Won't Get Fooled Again.

That's us.

Praise, not rage, is what Gospel Music was supposed to be about. But we had moved on. *Persecution Games* was moving into virgin territory. I can't imagine Gospel music going where we went next. The *Book of Lamentations* was my religion now. In a radio interview Robert said Galilee was more Blues than Praise. He told the interviewer that he drew his inspiration from the downbeat *Psalms of David*.

I wrote the words to *Fighting Man* in 1979 – 3 months before Hans Kung got sacked and 12 months before Des Ford. So it would be fair to say, I was pre-pissed off. Robert and Neale upped the ante in the studio, taking the anger in the lyrics to another level. When I heard the demos, I was exultant that they had maintained the rage, not muted it. Because they could have, of course - instead of reading it as a declaration of war-song, they could have created a 'fighting-man-I-never-was' impotent kinda song. But Neale was like a caged animal. He was never going to play impotent. And the mood Robert was in, plus rediscovering Sally and bringing her to Melbourne, all the shackles were off now.

Fighting Man is actually about self-condemnation – I am that narrow-minded Fighting Man. I have no love. Given a chance, I might have been Oliver Cromwell, tearing down the motifs of my enemies. Looking into the mirror and finding no peace in religion was the meaning of the words when I wrote them. And the band turned it into a monster:

> *I heard another Gospel, as wrong as wrong can be*
> *I act like an apostle, make the blind men see*

> *Shake em with your word, make them feel absurd*
> *Talk of love in anger, make em understand yer*
> *Jesus - can you love a fighting man?*

The song closes with Adolf Hitler haranguing his adoring throng.

The meaning of *Bureaucracy Blues* is threefold: yours, Robert's and mine...!

(1) ***You.*** Admit it. You're afraid to dissent - it could cost you your job, church friends, possibly your superannuation and maybe even your bloody social order. And who is to blame? The bureaucracy of course - you know that! Church administration has got absolutely nothing to do with Jesus, and all the stuff that appealed when you signed up for religion. You know that. The church admin is not dissimilar to Coles-Amatil. The CEOs even look interchangeable! 'Loving Jesus' does not = 'church'. Paying tithe, watching good people get sacked, investing in dodgy church-backed investments...ha ha har.

(2) ***Macrocosm.*** Robert (studying Sociology at the time) was thinking of Max Weber. He says, 'who a century ago put bureaucracy under the spotlight and didn't much like what he saw - mainly its irresistible denial of democracy and tendency to self-aggrandisement. Lowell was coming from his own space no doubt...'

Yeah, I was.

> *Don't say I ever loved you*
> *I never did, I never did at all*

(3) ***Microcosm.*** Expelled from Avondale College in 1970, and while not exactly 'kicked out' of teaching in 1978 - I might as well have been...! Angry? I'm just warming up!

Robert too got a dishonourable discharge from Avondale. In 1980 he was tutoring at Monash Uni. 1980 - that's when I got my Literature Grant- so we were all getting the message that the SDA system treats us like dirt, whereas the 'world' doesn't. Genna was doing all right too and Sally was finding her feet away from a church that was so reluctant of her accepting her talents - time to settle where we might be appreciated.

Approximately 1981-82 is when (to quote poet Allen Ginsberg),
I saw the best minds of my generation...
...leave the Church.

An architect, dentist, property developer, councillor, businesswoman, retailer, newsletter owner, English Master at Scots College, several doctors, a party plan saleswoman for enticing lingerie, New Zealand's pre-eminent sitar master, and so on.

They all walked out.

But, not Robert.

Years later I harkened back to 1982-1995 and said, 'Remember when we all became Atheists...?' *(In my case, I prefer 'Nihilist'.)*

Robert answered, 'Well, I was never that!'

Until the sacking of Des Ford, our third Galilee album was originally to be titled *King of the Ghettoes* and its sub-theme was Jesus as a Communist. That was my conclusion after listening to the well-politicised Robert, reading the gospels and coupled with my utter poverty as a fisherman.

Our response to the sacking of Des Ford is the song *Persecution Games*:

> *Let's get rid of Desmond, do it in the night*
> *Do it in a hurry, make sure you get it right...etc,*

...actually – believe it or not – it is not specifically about 'Desmond'. Desmond is just a 'type'. (As in 'type meets antitype' at theology school.)

To me, 'persecution' had become a very Christian theme. The pullout cover alludes to: Fox's *Book of Martyrs*, my 1973 play *Martin Luther,* the Azaria case, Tiny Tim, the Hara Krishna movement, the Salvation Army, the Beatles, and especially the June 1979 tragedy at Sydney's Luna Park.

The song *Vinegar* is the last song on the album.

To me, the **real** last song was *Bootleg Army*. I wrote it about the Streetpreachers, the people who had funded Galilee and made all this possible. The ragged army that pulled up the trailer every Sunday in Collins Street Melbourne for five years asking the question:

Is this the Kingdom, are we warriors now?

I revisited the theme in 2013:

> *We fought shoulder to shoulder, for our strange little cause*
> *From a fishing boat somewhere, miles from public applause*
>
> *We fought shoulder to shoulder, and I'd do it again*
> *Yes we were an army, and you were my friends*

The Persecution Games Cover/Artwork

As if Persecution Games wasn't already complex enough, we've got to go back to 1966 for the origins of the cover...the year I was in Dave Caldwell's Ancient History class, the year I heard the Cream song *Tales of Brave Ulysses*.

I didn't know Ancient History could be a Pop song, plus I noted the lyrics were by Australian, Martin Sharp who also designed the album cover *Disraeli Gears* and later, Cream's *Wheels of Fire* silver/gold double album cover.

Martin was a big Tiny Tim fan - so am I. Martin liked my interview with Tiny, which was published in the *Southern Flyer*. He invited me to stay at his Bellevue Hill house whenever I came to Sydney. Pretty soon we became friends and I kept coming back. Most nights we'd sit up way past midnight talking about all sorts of things, including the Azaria case and the 1979 Luna Park fire in which six children and one adult were killed. I played him some early *Persecution Games* demos, and talked about *Songs of Innocence/Experience* while he told me about Abraxas - the two faces of God. In time, this became the idea for the happy/sad cover of *Persecution Games*.

Martin was also fascinated by Sydney street-writer Arthur Stace, a reformed alcoholic who devoted his life to chalking the word 'Eternity' on Sydney streets in the pre-dawn hours, so the commuters would see that powerful word on their way to word. It is the most concise sermon ever preached. Martin wrote it on the back cover of *Persecution Games*.

Lowell: Sadly, Martin died 1 December 2013 and I miss him lots.

RULING CLASS
Lyrics - Lowell Tarling; Music - RW 1979

Am
Look at me Jesus
G Am
I'm a fisherman
C F G C
I been pulling my nets with a cold, cold hand
F
The wind comes up
C
The seas get rough
F C
Lord you know these times are tough
G E7 Am
But the ruling class gets on
G E Am
The ruling class gets on
Look at me Jesus I'm a trucking man
Driving my load all across the land
I sleep at night
All alone
Lord won't you care for my kids back home
The ruling class gets on
The ruling class gets on
Look at me Jesus I'm shifting sand
Sweating in my body
I've got a blistered hand
I been lifting logs and carrying stone
Trying to build my kids a home
The ruling class gets on
The ruling class gets on
Look at me Jesus
Look down if you can
Tell me that you feel for a working man
Do you believe in equality?
Why do the rich look down on me?
The ruling class gets on
The ruling class gets on

Robert: Loved these words too – I'd been a truckie for three years (1975-77) and a builder's labourer on and off while at Avondale and after (1971-74), and was right into reading Marx and other Left radicals while doing my BA in sociology and politics at this time (1978-1980). I never performed it anywhere, but it worked well with Mick and the band on the Persecution Games album.

Lowell: Verse 1 was for Bermagui – fishermen like Al, Keith, Titch. Verse two was for Robert. Verse 3 was for Robbie – we got a woman to sing the 'building' verse for that reason".

16
Damn Right, I Got the Blues

Neale Farnell

Bob explained that the Persecution Games album would have a 'soft' A-Side and a dark B-Side.

Bluesmeister Neale

Although my name is Neale Farnell, I sometimes go by Neale Swine. About the time we were working on *Persecution Games*, Robbie, Liz, Lowell, Nadene – a whole bunch of us - were in the back of Phil Ward's Range Rover driving to a Mick Reid gig in Tathra NSW. I pulled out a bottle of Old Kedge Rum and asked, 'Anyone wanna swig of the Old

Swine?' That's how I copped The Swine. Other times they call me Neale Vicious.

After that trip, when we got back to Bermagui, Lowell and his high school friend Allan Broadhurst wrapped a 7-piece band around me and called us the Swines. Aged 13, Dave Jensen was our sax player (later *Trout Fishing in Quebec*). His Dad Pete, the English Master from Scots College, was on vocals. Also on vocals, I recall Allan screeching through *Red House*, while I played a *veeecious* Hendrix leadbreak that blew everybody's ears out, in the little *Le Marlin Café*. But I'm getting way ahead of myself.

I didn't have the same religious background as Bob Wolfgramm, but I did have a religious background. Like Little Richard, Elvis and Aretha Franklin, church was where I first noticed music. But church music didn't exactly turn me on. I was a bad kid, anyway.

Then, when I was seven, I heard Jimi Hendrix's *Are You Experienced* LP. Being little, I didn't have the money to buy records, so I borrowed/pinched them off someone and from there I spent my teenage years listening to Buddy Guy, Johnny Winter and a lot of Blues-based Rock.

I got my first guitar when I was 13. It was a cheap Japanese acoustic and I carried it everywhere. Some of the bigger kids had a school band. They played songs that I liked/hated. Later, I became one of the big kids, but by then I'd learned how to play pretty well. I formed my first band in high school. We played the school concert.

I first met Bob Wolfgramm in 1977 when I was 17. I was invited to a band audition (by bass player Doug Saunders). It was held upstairs at his digs in Burgundy Street Heidelberg. At that audition I also met guitarist Greg Hughson, mouth harpist Colin Mack and John Rigby on vocals and keyboards. I got the gig!

The band was called *Passport*, and Bob was on vocals. We rehearsed songs like Bob Marley's *I Shot the Sheriff*, Joe Cocker's *You Are So Beautiful* and an assortment of Jazz-Rock songs that I simply can't remember. But I wasn't quite sure what Bob was doing there. He didn't seem to enjoy singing and seemed happiest playing rhythm guitar away from the limelight.

The penny dropped at one rehearsal when Bob introduced us to a couple of songs he'd written, *Look A-Yonder* and *Two of Me Walking in One Man Blues*. So that's what he is – a songwriter!

Passport played a few gigs at Mont Park Asylum (supposedly haunted) and Larundel Mental Hospital.

After that, Bob and I started hanging out a bit more. I met his wife Ag, daughters Kelly and Talei, and baby Eliza. Bob showed me a couple of Gospel albums that he'd made and talked a lot about wanting to get back to the studio. I wasn't used to seeing him this animated, so I organized getting *Passport* into the *BB Rolls Studios* in Abbotsford and we recorded a few Bob Wolfgramm songs, including one called *Look A-Yonder*.

The photos on Bob's website were taken during these sessions.

Passport eventually evolved into another line up. John and Doug dropped out, drummer Lee Davidson joined, as did bassist Con Campinello. I suppose Bob dropped out too. He was a university tutor now, a father of three, plus he had other musical projects to pursue.

One day, while sitting on his verandah at Ferntree Gully and watching his goat, Robert started talking about *Persecution Games*, a Gospel album idea with a lot of bite to it. Songs with words like *I wanna be a fighter for the Lord* - in which he wanted my input. I told him there's only one way I know with songs like that: he should lay down a rhythm track to create a feel, then I'll come in with the Stratocaster and stick a spear up the song's arse. *Veeecious*. I wasn't sure if he'd like that, but apparently he did.

Bob explained that the *Persecution Games* album would have a 'soft' A-Side and a dark B-Side. He wanted to use Mick Reid's Sydney band for Side A and our new line-up on Side B. After that, I went home and arranged the songs on our Stratocaster side while Bob was in Sydney recording the Telecaster side.

Eventually we started recording at studios in Glenhuntly. Sally

Hilder came to Melbourne to lay down some vocals on songs like *King of the Ghettoes*, *Bootleg Army* and few others. So, I got to know Sally.

Later I went to Sydney to finish off a few guitar tracks at Riverwood Studios (suburb). That's where I met fiddle player Mike Kerin and the pedal steel player from the *Slim Dusty Band*. After that, we called on Slim's guitarist Mick Reid at his Blue Mountains home. But best of all, I also visited Kings Cross where I did my best to get us all into trouble. I had a great time in Sydney.

Also on that trip I met Genna. We argued straight away because he asked too many personal questions about my relationship with Liz. As for Lowell - we'd met some time before on Bob's verandah at the Ferntree Gully house. We also argued. He just wouldn't shut up about the singer Tiny Tim.

This was just the beginning of a continuing friendship with Bob, Lowell, Genna and Sally - and a cast of about another 35 people associated with *Persecution Games* and *Galilee Music*. Colin Mack and I have continued performing in various blues bands ever since, most notably *Drowning on Dry Land*. We've played pubs, bars, biker rallies – everywhere where audiences love down-the-line hard rocking blues.

Persecution Games was released mid-1985. After that we were soon back in the studio. Half our time was spent arranging songs for Tina Arena with Mike Bikicki for which we were paid in studio hours. So Bob and I worked on his new songs, like *God of Shadows*, *Questioning the Plan* and *Iron Lady*.

What I have written is a brief account of only the first part of a continuing productive musical journey. Thirty-six years later, 2013 sees the start of a new project with Bob and me, made possible by new technology which allows us to record in our respective home studios (him in Fiji, me in Melbourne) and email the tracks back and forth.

With Bob, who knows where's it's going? Maybe a new Galilee Record?

Or maybe it's just for fun, because we're friends.

BUREAUCRACY BLUES
Lyrics - Lowell Tarling; Music - RW 1979

Em
You get just what you pay for
You pay in blood and bone
Am Em
You pay and you trample on everyone you own
Me you see me running
You'll get me in the end
Bm7 Cmaj7
Don't say I ever loved you
F#m7
I never was
Fmaj Em
I never was your friend
You're sharp
So very cutting
You cut some people down
Select them and use them
And then you grind them down
Me I know your number
But I'm so very small
Don't say I ever loved you
I never did at all

Robert: Undoubtedly the punkiest, angriest song I've ever collaborated on with Lowell. He was coming from his own space no doubt, whereas I was coming to terms with Max Weber, the German co-founder of sociology who a century ago put bureaucracy under the spotlight and didn't much like what he saw – mainly, its irresistible denial of democracy and tendency to self-aggrandisement.

17

Apocalypse Riders, 1998

Malachi Doyle

I have my faith, but I don't really like talking about it. For me words get in the way. But singing those songs was a revelation.

Malachi

The first *Apocalypse Rider* show was at Monash University in Frankston. I was battling glandular fever and had spent the previous two weeks in bed. But the show must go on. And Robert - who'd put the thing together had done so much for me in my life: introducing me to the world of Sociology, the history of ideas, the world of his indigenous Fiji, and most importantly for me the history of 20th century popular music - needed me. And boy, did I believe in the music: existential Gospel music, music that spoke from personal experience, not platitudes falling over each other in balloons of praise. Sure, there's a place for that, for some, but for me, at 27, I wanted to hear Fijian-Tongan stories, Australian stories. Stories of struggles inside faith.

So the night began. The sweats were with me everywhere, but so was the excitement, the camaraderie, and a building crowd. Unlike every other gig I'd played till that point, I had complete belief in the material. The songs were incredible. Literate, truthful and really, really catchy. & I was the luckiest one there, coz I got to sing *It Was News To Me*, a song the term 'power ballad' had been coined for. I felt the words as I sang, 'my hands and feet have wandered, his hands and feet were nailed... and he died for my failures before I was born'. I don't think I've ever sung a song with more feeling just by reading the words. It's the best gospel song I've ever heard. A joy to be there.

The rest of the show was a bit of a blur as my fever hit. Images of Lowell with his bodhran and Terry on his steel guitar. I think I got up to sing *The Storm*. What is that? A love song or a Gospel song? Does it matter? God can be found in the arms of a lover. I loved standing side by side off the drum kit for a few minutes next to Robert. Joined in battle. A bond that lasts for life. Actually the more I think about it the more I remember. Kelly's bruised, beautiful rendition of *Save Your Grace*, Talei powerfully bluesying with Chris Russell on *War n Hate n Trouble*.

Apocalypse Rider

It was great just to hit the drum skins, sing a few harmonies and listen to all the wonderful words and performances. The all-singing-all-playing band is a special thing. A bastard beast whose beauty is richer for its many facets. Had we have made a studio record we would have smashed it. That was a good band. That was an amazing band. All come together for the love and respect of Robert. A king amongst men. A family of blood and water. A motley crew, as gospellers are best to be. I just wish we'd made a studio album. If only someone had some bloody money! Still the memories are sweet. Always exciting to see Lowell. They broke the mould when they made him.

I first met Robert Wolfgramm when I was studying Sociology at Chisholm College (later Monash Uni) in Frankston. We chatted briefly about Bob Dylan and I think Tom Petty. He said, 'drop by anytime' to his office for a chat. I'd never met such a cool teacher before – great hair, great shirt, winning smile – he knew who he was and had style – and I told my musical friend Terry McCarthy who was studying with me.

Before long we'd hang out after classes with guitars and kava (which Robert introduced us to) at Robert and Lupe's place near campus. We'd trade stories and tunes and Robert would pull out records from his expansive collection. Among these were an album with Robert on the cover simply titled *Bob* and one by Sally - someone who sang like an angel - called *All My Friends Are Sinners*. I didn't sort of realize that this was religious music. Sure there were biblical references, but the music didn't have the usual saccharine sound and platitudinous lyrics. I loved the stuff and Robert invited me to sing some of the songs, which he recorded on his little 4-track. We were just jamming. I was very green and didn't imagine that we'd ever get a band together and play the Adventist College in Cooranbong and have a choir behind us and all that. I was all ears and feelings and soaking life in like a sponge. I had no serious plans. I guess I was young and really un-driven.

The whole thing happened very organically, our friendship was the main thing and that generated everything. Eventually we introduced more of our friends like Chris Rose and Chris Russell to Robert. It all stemmed from 'Bob's Café' every Friday night. It's funny how we ended up playing for a Christian audience even though none of us were particularly religious. I think I referred to us - the band - as 'a pack of heathens'. But anyway, we believed in Robert and Lowell, who was probably the most interesting person I'd ever met - sort of intimidated me but excited me with his art knowledge and joie de vie.

First came friendship, then came the *Bula Brothers* (our Fijian language jam band), then came the *Apocalypse Rider* musical. In between came a trip to Fiji. My first time overseas and a life changing experience, my introduction to the developing world, my introduction to communal living, village life and making your fun from what you had. No (or limited) electricity, no TVs, homemade entertainment. And that spirit Robert brought to everything. What I grew up in my Irish Catholic family to know as the 'amateur spirit'. Not doing something because it's gonna make you money, but because the event will be great. I s'pose it's very Hippy, though I think equally Punk - the 'do it yourself' thing. Yeah. Celebration of friendship, music, the body, the mind. I think Jesus would be pleased. God would rejoice in the dance.

I mean it's a pretty gutsy thing to get up and say, '*I don't agree with everything you guys say. My faith is personal and it goes like this, and I mean it with love, but maybe you won't agree with all of it, but maybe you'll like some of it, but certainly you will feel it. Feel the sincerity of it. This is about God, my God*'. I don't have the confidence in my words to say all that. I have my faith, but I don't really like talking about it. For me words get in the way. But singing those songs was a revelation. I might walk around thinking this and that, be a bit scattered – particularly when I was younger – but the minute I sang those songs, for the length of the song, boom! I was fully there. Total conviction.

The rest of the time, I'm not so sure, but good Gospel music is that like that: during the life of the song you are filled with faith. And it sustains you. It helps you. Like meditation does. Positive stuff. It counteracts all the negative shit. Don't preach to me, *sing* to me. And not platitudes, something you really think, having dug deep inside yourself to find.

The other thing about Robert and Lowell is not just their sincerity and truthfulness, is that they are intelligent and full of energy & they give. They work hard. And they're organized. Lyrics and chords all printed out. Easy. Thank you. I'm on the train trying to write this on my phone. I'll redraft tomorrow.

Sydney. Avondale. Year: 1999.

All of us on the bus: the heathens the band, the choir from some youth group, miscellaneous believers and Robert the leader with family. We set out in the afternoon and into the night. I sat next to my then wife who was really great to be with coz Robert organised special accommodation for us - with the college caretaker and his wife. We had luxury accommodation compared to the rest of the band, who had been given the college dorm for the night, haha.

Time for the historic concert had come. My wife and I sat down to dinner with the college people. I think there was a youth camp or something on at the college at the time. There were lots of believers around... but no band!

I started to worry. Sat around and chatted with Robert and Lupe and the kids. Where were the bloody heathens!? Opening time beckoned and Robert must have felt like a missionary of sorts, with his band of unconventionals about to stand before the college that had schooled Lowell and him all those decades before. He'd left the church for a while, but now he was back.

The musicians among us left their loved ones: Calvin, Robert, me and Robert's daughters yeah, and the choir, that's right, went back stage. We could hear the audience start to build in this American-style timber terraced two-storey 19th century time warp design by the prophet of Adventism no less. Tension ... and by now a bit of anger, about the whereabouts of Matt (Nees), Chris, Terry and Phil (Carr) ... when they finally walk in stinking of alcohol. Back from the pub with halos about them and smiles on their faces.

I barely looked at them as Robert and the vocal quartet and the leader of the choir blessed us all with a pre match prayer. I thought, 'You bastards! you're gonna let us down!' I needn't have worried.

Then, walking out into darkness. Robert's spoken intro to the room of the faithful. He mentioned something about his Polynesian heritage and the importance of drums to his people. I believe this was the first time drums had been played in that sacred venue and we had two drummers!

We start: Crash! And wow, the acoustics almost otherworldly. What a 'live' room! The sound travelled away from you at the speed of light and left you way behind. And the drunken band? Perfection! This was Aussie pub rock music with heavenly vocals. What a marriage of contrasts. William Blake would be proud. Bitchin' Rock n Roll with Gospel lyrics. The crowd was sort of speechless at first, but then really warmed up. They loved it. Most of em anyway, haha.

The highlight for me came when Chris and Talei did *War and Hate and Trouble*. Talei sang powerful blues from the guts as usual, and then Chris' solo came. Picture Angus Young playing the same two notes for 6-8 bars. Drone and bend. I'm thinking is he ever gonna change? when finally at the death knell, he lets go a delicate flurry of notes to complete the sequence. By the time the acapella four sang, we had the crowd of believers (if doubters of us, the look of us) eating out if our hands. Robert brought it all home with *Look a Yonder* – the rewrite of Richie Havens song? 'I saw people and they were free, standing in the waters of Galilee'.

Too right. They were free at that moment. I have no doubt.

Apocalypse Rider performance; Avondale College Chapel 1999

IT WAS NEWS TO ME
Lyrics - Lowell Tarling; Music - RW 1978

G Am7 - C
It was news to me
Cm7 G
It was already done
Em Asus - A
Before my birth
Am D
It had been won
It could not be earned
Before I was born
On Jesus shoulders
He carried my scorn
[Ref:]
C
He carried my cross in silence
G D G7
I should have walked that trail
C
My hands and feet have wandered
A D7
His hands and feet were nailed
G Am7 - C
My head has been turned
Cm7 G
His crowned with thorns
Em Asus - A Am - D G
And he died for my failures before I was born
It was news to me

Born at a cost
We were all found
When he was lost
Sometimes I hear that God is dead
But the death of God, my God
Makes me bow my head

Robert: Some of my favourite Lowell words ever – economically didactic and says it all. An honour to be given them to do something with. I sang it a bit at street- preacher Bible studies and a version of it is on my Bob-Refugee album. Ivan and the Caldwell family also did a version on the album. Malachi Doyle did it justice too when he sang it in the Apocalypse Rider.

Anne and Genna, 1980

18

Support Act

Anne Levitch

We all had great respect for the creative spirit in each other, our partners, our families and the Galilee 'family'.

Ag and Anne at the launch of All My Friends Are Sinners

We grew up in a conservative Adventist milieu. As we came of age, those of us who questioned the righteous elitism of the church and the strict religiosity were drawn together naturally. We were the fringe dwellers and had each other for company. It was a natural consequence that Galilee grew out of this.

Music was an acceptable medium to provide a voice for the building spirit of rebellion while not being too confronting.

Lying awake at first light and listening to the cacophony of birds as dawn was breaking this morning seemed the perfect experience to trigger my mental musings on Galilee and spiritual tolerance. So many different 'voices' all totally different, from screeching cockatoos to chirping king parrots, squawking miners, warbling currawongs and tweeting sparrows plus many more. Some with piercing songs, some backing 'vocals', some harmony, but all together contributing to the celebration of a common experience of daybreak. If the hundreds of birds had one voice, daybreak would not be heralded in such passionate form.

That is what Galilee was like. A record label that enabled many different voices to come together and express religious and spiritual experience. The best thing was the honest expression of joy, angst, frustration, challenge, peace, anger, connection and disconnection. It was very sad and telling, that the church had difficulty with that honesty.

As Christian music at this time was so heavily represented by the pure, sweet and loving Christian experience to the point of nausea, the Galilee voice was refreshing.

We recently attended the 2013 Australian Songwriters Awards and I shuddered when the winning song in the Gospel category was nothing but the same elevator schmaltz that we had walked away from over 40 years ago!

The Galilee songs had honest rawness and depth, avoiding the superficiality of being all 'nice' gospel songs. I felt a bit distant as the songs on first and second albums were still primarily about the journey of faith, belief, and redemption. I felt they could have gone much further, but it was a great start, a different voice coming from the soil of a deeply conservative religion and I could celebrate that with them. The third album was more challenging of the hierarchy and the church.

I took Genna's car one day during early Galilee years and as the car started, *Missionary Man* by Annie Lennox started playing. I thought it was the tape of a recent Galilee recording and was excited they were breaking new ground. I was wrong, but *Persecution Games* touched that space for many people. Galilee music was always based around faith, not disbelief. I felt like an outsider as I had well and truly left religion by this time. While I respected what Galilee was doing, I did not feel the need to challenge the church. I had just walked away.

I was often blamed for taking Genna out of the church. He had been a golden boy, a strong believer, school captain, street preacher, and actively engaged in church life. I was a quiet fringe dweller with one foot in and one foot out from age 14, when I spent weekends with good friends outside of the church milieu debating, dancing, and listening to 'non' Christian music. We finally met through Salt events; however, we had attended the same church school where I thought he was a bit righteous and arrogant. He gave my friend and I, a lift one day and we just chatted easily together. We left the church within a year kept each other company in our waywardness. Many of our old friends were still there, but we spent more and more time away from church gatherings.

I had known Lowell and Robert from time at the same high school, although we were all in different years. At the time the Galilee 'boys' were working on the albums, I was living the 'two of me walking in one man blues' literally and loved that song as it gave voice to the feeling. While I had walked away from Adventism some years before, I was living proof that I could take the girl away from Adventism, but I was having trouble taking Adventism away from the girl. It took me years of personal growth to challenge and become aware of the deeply entrenched beliefs, which I had absorbed between pulpit and schoolroom. I still do battle with myself when I recognise reactions that are still influenced by these inculcated childhood beliefs.

I grew to know Lowell a little better when Genna had a very minor role in *Jonah* the musical. We commiserated when Genna managed to 'drag focus' with his two words of script. We note his tendency to do this has not diminished over the decades since!

As Galilee wives, we all danced to a different drum. Ag Wolfgramm was raised in an Adventist offshoot movement, Robbie Tarling in England where Adventism had little influence, and I, in mainstream Aussie Adventism. We had all fashioned our own beliefs in adulthood, and respected each other. We supported our husbands at the time, unconditionally, in whatever way we could. We all respected the effort it took to create and bring together the lyrics, the music, the band, the recording, and the physical product at completion.

For Robbie and Ag, it was a more difficult time as they were juggling the demands of young families and indulged their husbands' commitment to Galilee and the need for time away. We all had great respect for the creative spirit in each other, our partners, our families and the Galilee 'family'. We have all continued in careers and pursuits in creative industries. A strong bond of shared experience and respect and open honesty has continued throughout our lives.

In my thirties, I was able to separate my disrespect of religion from my spirituality. Religion does not attract me in any form. However, I have respect for anyone on a spiritual path and I continue to hone my own eclectic framework of beliefs. Adventism was too elitist for me and too arrogant in saying that it has 'The Truth'. I still have dear old friends who remained in the church and we respect each other's paths. However, Adventism, at core, is not known to have respect for other beliefs, and there are many.

The world is an exciting and tolerant place for those of us 'born from original sin' - in fact, come to think of it...all my friends *are* sinners!

19
Of Music, Mice & Men

Dr Robert Wolfgramm

Department of Sociology Monash University 1999

Cultural expression is neither a priori good nor bad, moral nor immoral.

Sally and Robert, Newcastle 2013

What follows is a critique of prejudices against contemporary popular music.

These prejudices against both gospel and secular pop music are pervasive within Adventism and are typically reflected in a 1999 special issue of the American journal, *Adventists Affirm (AA)*. Since this particular special issue has been widely endorsed and advertised in the official South Pacific SDA church paper, *The Record*, one may reasonably conclude that it has the imprimatur of the Division brethren and sisters.

I intend to argue against the writers of the *Adventist Affirm* special issue, that contemporary popular music is no more good or evil than the popular music of any previous generation, and that it too will fade into the annals of the late 20thcentury kitsch culture. I will also argue that their prejudices against it stem from inadequate research and are poorly considered in that they are too generalised, and too rooted in an unreflexive cultural absolutism.

Before taking up my critique of their positions, I would like to first outline the basis of my commitment to the subject of contemporary popular music (1) and my passion for it (2).

Of Music - my musical education

Like many Pacific islanders, I was affected by music early in life because it was in the family and perhaps 'in the blood' (as they say). My father's brother, Bill Wolfgramm, was already a steel-guitar recording star when I was born in 1952.

My own father was apparently a terrific pianist. As early as 1948, Bill's records with his *Islanders* (a guitar-based ensemble) were popular in the Pacific and I grew up listening to them in my Tongan grandfather's home in Fiji. Alongside these were scratchy 78s of Jimmie Rogers, Jim Reeves, Hank Williams snr, Patsy Cline, and a small field of other achy-breaky cowboy yodellers. The only other music form I was really exposed to (apart from church hymns and 'Elim' choruses) was brass band music. Sometimes, when a cruise ship approached Suva harbour, my grandfather would take me down to see the boat come alongside as the brass band of the Fiji military or police forces played.

I learned to sing in Sabbath school and to play a ukulele in primary school, in Fiji, at about six years of age. The primary school headmaster, Mr Williams, ran us through a two-chord wonder called, *Won't You Play A Simple Melody*. I then heard these same two chords, D and A7, in many cowboy songs my relatives sang around our family home. When they chimed in and taught me a third chord, G, it seemed the whole world of popular music was suddenly and literally at my fingertips.

Then, after my uncle Eddie turned up with his guitar one day and sang the Jim Reeves classic, *He'll Have To Go* - chord for chord, note for note, inflection for inflection - I just about fell over with joy. I recognised how accessible music was and how possible it was to be Jim Reeves.

When I commenced schooling in Australia in 1964, my interest in music was minimal but I thought there were only two instruments in the world that mattered - ukulele (which I could play) and the guitar (which the Beatles played). That was until I came to live as a boarder with the family of Adventist teacher and musician, Dave Caldwell. He insisted I take up an instrument and that I learn to read music.

So I did, hymns and marches, mostly through learning to play (appropriately enough) a brass band instrument - the B-flat bass, and then the E-flat bass. I learned about transposition and was a member of the Advent Brass band in Sydney for three years. Once a week, Lance Butler picked me up from Pymble and took me to practices at Strathfield. I had the privilege of marching twice in Anzac Day parades, of playing in rotundas, at church functions and in competitions in the Sydney Town Hall.

I also learned to play 'by ear' during this time through playing ukulele at Adventist folk music jams ('hootenannies') which were popular in Sydney's North Shore circles. The first song I figured out 'by ear' on the ukulele was the Beatles', *I Should Have Known Better*. I heard this while on school holidays in Honiara (the capital of the Solomon Islands). After that, I bought sheet music when I could afford it, copied songs from songbooks and listened to records very closely to discover the structure of the song - to this day I cannot sing the words to most 60s songs but I know how to play them!

Despite not owning one, I then took up teaching myself guitar in 1967 and left the brass band at about the same time. Lowell Tarling and an Indian Adventist fellow called Louis Rao were my immediate inspirations and models.

I was amazed at how good-looking young girls seemed to be attracted not only to the Beatles but to Lowell and Louis. The first song I learned and sang on guitar was, like millions of others, Eric Burdon's version of *House of the Rising Sun* - a song about a brothel as it turned out.

In 1968, I began at Lilydale Academy and formed a band with friends. Using hired amplifiers and bass guitar, we won the Warburton SDA church talent quest playing an instrumental cover of the Beatles' drug song, *Daytripper*.

Pastor Parr handed us the prize. The song was entirely consistent with my reputation at Lilydale as a 'druggie' - a reputation based on speculative rumours about my tired and shabby appearance. But I was an utter stranger to drugs having had nothing stronger than a Bex and a good lie down. Being deprived of outside cultural stimulation, my fatigue mostly derived from the fact that my only source of music came from many a night propped up awkwardly in fellow-boarder, Phillip Wallace's clothes cupboard listening to 3XY on a crystal-set he had smuggled into the place and had hidden away.

All transistor radios were banned at Lilydale at that time and even my vinyl records had been confiscated - and cheerily destroyed (against his word) by the deputy principal who went on to become a Union Conference administrator. To compensate for these deprivations, I thereby played guitar and piano with whomever, whenever, wherever I could - duets, trios, quartets; covers and originals, in Australia and Fiji.

I also compensated by trying my hand at songwriting. The first songs I wrote (aged 15) were Dylan-inspired protest songs and Beatles-inspired love songs. Then, encouraged by suggestions from friends like Ivan Caldwell, Col Osman, Pauline Crawford, and Andrew Kingston, I started writing Christian-experience songs (aged 16). Then (aged 19), at the behest of people like Lowell Tarling, Terry Wilkinson and Peter McDougall, I began to write more Biblically-based gospel message songs.

In 1971, while at Avondale, I worked with Lowell as co-lyricist. We wrote and produced a contemporary-style folk-cantata we called *Threedom*. Peter McDougall hired me for the holidays and believed in me so much, he paid me to score it. Alan Thrift was a tremendous support also, but the College 'heavies' were very worried about it. They formed a special music committee to ensure that it lived up to Adventist values. Pastor Arch Hefren got right to the point when he called me into his office and told me point blank, 'Robert, you are the Devil's disciple'. Dr Noel Pavitt Clapham would sit through rehearsals and make notes which would turn up in my mail as the committee's suggestions for improving the cantata.

This censorship notwithstanding, we eventually performed it with a small ensemble of about 20 singers and players during the years 1971-72 in Newcastle and in Sydney. After its Avondale premiere, Doc Clapham at least had the good grace to seek me out, shake my hand and squintingly tell me he thought I had the musical gifts of at least a Schumann, if not a Schubert. Despite its uniqueness, public interest and positive critical reception, no offer was ever made to record *Threedom*.

At that time Lowell and I were also regular starters as 'Streetpreachers' in Sydney, Melbourne, Newcastle and other centres. As Streetpreachers, we not only witnessed through personal testimonies and group singing on city streets, we took on the job of writing and performing original Christian songs for the occasions. Lowell and I also gigged in coffee-shop poetry readings with Bev Wilkinson, as well as at various church-organised functions.

By 1977, our songs were being sung and shared among Streetpreachers and youth groups in Melbourne and in Sydney.

One street-preaching 'high' included Mark 'Chopper' Read coming to my rescue when, provoked by a trio of racist Heil-Hitler-ing Nazis in full uniform, I completely lost the plot. Another high was thrashing out Jesus Blues with my hero Lowell Tarling, with drummer Bill Smith, mouth-harpist Colin Mack and bassist Carl Needham.

The highs also included meeting a bevy of enthusiastic and searching street youth at Peter and Jenny McDougall's Bible studies, through Jim Johanson's East Prahran Church, and through the youth ministries of Adrian Jones, the Kingston and the Coombs' families.

Robert & Carl Needham (Carl designed Sally and Bob's albums and the Galilee logo)

As a consequence of these encounters, many thought the songs I had written for the street mission were worth recording, and this time I was naïve enough to approach the brethren in Wahroonga and the Adventist Media Centre (ARTP as it was called) for a record deal.

Warren Judd, who had some influence there and had encouraged my songwriting and had earlier recorded three of my compositions and arrangements on church-sponsored albums, politely told me of the brethren's view that I should forget it: there was no money in the kitty for my product, and who did I think would want to buy it? Meanwhile, the range of the church's sponsored artists was incredibly 'safe' and narrow.

Through no fault of Judd, church contemporary music productions looked more and more like a family business - the church label featured records by Judd, his wife, his brother, his sister-in-law and their friends.

Eventually, Lowell - who had been writing and producing Sydney-based oratorio-plays of his own - *Martin Luther* and *Jonah* - introduced me to a student at Strathfield SDA high school where he was teaching. Her name was Sally Hilder and her voice, for a 15-year old, was stunning.

Over the Christmas-New Year period of 1977-78, with funding from Melbourne Streetpreachers and help from a number of Christian and non-Christian friends and musos, Paul Bryant recorded a first album (on vinyl and cassette) of Tarling-Wolfgramm gospel songs. Sally was our feature vocalist. And together with friend and financial adviser, Genna Levitch, we launched Galilee Records.

In early 1978, Sally's album, *All My Friends Are Sinners* - a title derived in my mind from Romans 5: 8 - was released through Spotlight Records - a trailblazing non-denominational Sydney-based Christian music distributor.

Sally's album was our debut in the 'contemporary Christian music scene'. And the first for an Adventist outfit in this country. Despite being unable to promote it on the road, Sally's album was critically well-received by both Christian reviewers and secular reviewers (one of whom said it set a new high in professionalism for a Christian recording). It made it onto several radio station playlists in Melbourne and Sydney. The album sold out in Christian circles. The early Christian contemporary music magazine *Keystone* and the Christian issues magazine, *On Being*, were particularly supportive of our work running our advertisements and doing interviews.

That encouraged us (Galilee and the Streetpreachers) to do more and in 1978-79 my solo album *Bob* (ie. *Refugee)* was recorded and released. Despite giving a number of well-received live performances at Christian venues to promote the album, I sold only a handful.

Again, *Keystone* and the Rhema organisation were tremendously helpful in publicity and in giving me exposure through their concert programs. I also had the privilege to meet and play with Australian secular artists who, out there in the pop music scene of the 60s and early 70s, came to discover Jesus and the awesome power of his gospel in their own journeys. Some have stayed with the path; others have moved on. But I think here of people like Barry Smith and Sam Dunnin/Melamed (ex-Town Criers from Melbourne), Harry Herni and Phil Carr (ex-Harts from Adelaide). There are others also.

In the summer of 1979-80, again funded by Streetpreachers, I went back into the studio with Sally Hilder and friends and recorded a final album, *Persecution Games*, a concept-protest-album developed with

Lowell Tarling.

Pop-artist Martin Sharp who had worked with Eric Clapton and his 60s psychedelic group Cream donated the cover art. In our view (which I still hold to), this was far and away the best work we had produced. Yet, as predicted by our financial adviser, the album sold least well of all as early 80s Christians were unsure of what to make of its bittersweet lyric and metal-aggro attitude.

My bands on those occasions (live and in the studio) were friends and hired professionals (who became friends) who contributed not only their musical gifts but much in terms of camaraderie and advice. They also shared their unique historical and cultural insights into the local Aussie music scene. More importantly, they encouraged me to think of my own music as an independent and distinctively 'Australian' contribution to Christian music discourse. They helped me to press on and make my own statement regardless of the orthodoxies and conventions, which defined the conservative Christian music 'sound'. This didn't always pay off but it has left me with accomplishments I look back on with great pride.

In each case, the point of my recorded work and performance was to document, hopefully for the betterment of others, my Christian convictions and beliefs as they had developed during my years as an Adventist streetpreacher. The point was not to be a star or to make profits but to make enough money to allow the ministry to proceed. And for seven years it did! In the end, I feel very privileged to have had great friends who, led by God, gave me many opportunities to share my spiritual songs and ideas and to eventually put them in hard copy form into the public domain. While I was disappointed with the Adventist church for refusing to stock our albums ('too way out') or to even note our 'fringe' ministry in its publications, I was flattered that someone 'out there' found Tarling-Wolfgramm important enough to include us in the *Who's Who of Australian Rock*!

Finally, a couple of Anglican ministers who are presently researching and authoring a book on the history of contemporary Christian music in Australia were delighted to make contact with me and to be able to document my 'front-line' (their words) involvement in contemporary Christian music ministry in this country.

Of Mice

Thirty years ago, when I first began writing songs, it was tomatoes; now it is mice. The tomatoes were reputedly fed a diet of classical music and were plump and yummy; more recently, hapless mice were fed a diet of 'Rock' music and ended up scrawny and insane. Thirty years ago 'Rock' was a Communist plot to corrupt Western Christian youth; now it is a Satanic plot. Thirty years ago it I was handed a copy of Bob Larson's hysterical *Rock and the Church* (3) and told to read it; now it is *Adventists Affirm* (4).

Can we go forward by standing still? The contributors to this edition of *AA* seem to think so (5). Theirs is another re-run of the conservative theme that Christians have a duty to reject the popular music of their times. I doubt that anyone young out there is still listening to this line of argument. But were they, I suspect the hopes of these Adventist writers would be dashed. Those who have sought to dislocate Christian praxis from the musical ethos of the times (and places) in which they have found themselves have invariably ended up listening only to the sound of their own applause.

My task here then, is to briefly deal with the familiar arguments against contemporary pop music as rehearsed by these contemporary Adventist thinkers. Along the way I will allude to some alternative orientations for a contemporary music criticism.

I: The Root Argument

One author tells us that the 'Christianised culture of sixteenth-century Europe' helped set down 'the rules of good music'. Another argues that the golden era of classical music is 1750-1830 because it is 'orderly' in nature. No explanation needed. No apology for this Eurocentrism, no theory of history, no definitions provided, no rationale for this preference - just bald statements. But what is a 'Chistianised culture'?

Where in 16th or 18th century Europe did it exist?

Writer, Louis Torres conversely asserts that 'polyrhythmical music had its roots in the pagan worship of Africa', specifically in 'voodoo' worship. The impression therefore is that Christian music derived from Europe is good; Christian music derived from Africa (if that is possible) is bad. No sense is given that Europe has been (or still is) pagan. No impression that forms of European 'voodoo' are extant. No appreciation of indigenous African music. Just a crude conflation of culture into morality with a racist sub-text.

One author approvingly cites Wolfgang Stefani's doctoral thesis where the latter makes the argument that music reflects moral culture. But where (one hopes) Stefani probably said something more sophisticated in relation to this, his argument is here turned into an arrow. The author notes that since pre-Christian sub-Saharan music was typically marked by participatory singing, clapping and dancing to the accompaniment of 'loud drums, heavy rhythms, complex chords and emotionally dramatic climaxes' this is something Christians should avoid. Guilt by association (6) - no self-reflection; no definition of terms; no comparative analysis. Certainly no mention of models of noisy participatory, celebratory Old or New Testament worship styles which may be adopted; just a crude apophetic argument using selectively convenient 'evidence' - again African.

Should a music form be rejected because of the human characteristics (pagan or otherwise) of its authors? Just what is the relationship between the human writer and the written output? If we are to reject 'Rock' because its authors and conveyors are demonstrably pagan or decadent - our premise being that an artist's lifestyle contaminates their art - then we had better examine every music and art form we privilege to make sure we are consistent. On these grounds, many of the 'great' composers preferred by the *AA* contributors would not, like Mick Jagger, pass muster.

For example, when listening to Bach's glorious *Easter Cantata*, do these opponents of Pop ignore the fact of his obsessive belief in numerology? Do they try not to think of him thrashing one of 23 children for not performing up to scratch on the family organ? Handel - who chose to be an Englishman - was the most religious of classical composers and some of us measure all oratorios against his *Messiah* but when singing its *Hallelujah Chorus* should we not think of him duelling in public with jealous rivals? When enraptured by Mozart's *Magic Flute* we must try not think of it - as he did - as a metaphor for his penis and his tribute to Freemasonry. Nor ought we think of his licentiousness and foul mouth (brought on we know now by his suffering Tourette's syndrome). When captured by the cadences of Schubert's 'Unfinished' Symphony do not to think of his hedonism and final syphilitic condition. So too, Beethoven, whose *Ode to Joy* is undoubtedly a masterpiece, but best appreciated without thinking of his lack of personal hygiene, his belief in numerology, his rabid womanising and his eventual degeneration due to syphilis. So too, when next listening to Berlioz you may choose to ignore his opium addiction but perhaps remember that his famous *Symphonie Fantastique* depicts a witchcraft seduction at black sabbath orgy.

Then again, the piano music of Schumann and Chopin may thrill you but put to one side the former's drunken larrikinism, promiscuity and eventual madness, and the latter's questionable (from the Christian *AA* point of view) sexuality. When next exhilarated by Wagner's *Tannahuser* we must try not to think of the anti-Semitic ideology behind his writing, and his being an out and out racist in that regard. Brahms' violin concerto may thrill the *AA* authors as it does me but we will ignore his philanderous affair with Clara Schumann while hubby Robert was institutionalised due to a nervous breakdown. Dvorak's American experience produced a glorious *New World Symphony* and vehement denial of charges of plagiarism in establishing its melodic theme - but we now know otherwise. Tchaikowsky has to my mind written the most romantic piano concerto ever but (if we are *AA* authors) we will try not think of his idea of romance as being fiercely homosexual. And Puccini's emotionally charged and unfinished *Turandot* is a highlight in my collection, but should I throw it out because he was shocker of a husband - his unfaithfulness responsible for at least one suicide?

But despite the apparent pagan debauchery of their classical greats, the *AA* authors seem particularly troubled that contemporary music has 'pagan' (ie. read African) antecedents. But if it is the paganism that worries them (rather than the specifically African source), they must know, even a cursory knowledge of anthropology, sociology and history divulges a whole range of 'pagan' antecedents not merely for contemporary popular music but for just about every other cultural practice we enjoy. For example, the beds we sleep on are originally a pagan Iranian idea. Our cotton sheets are pagan Indian and linen pagan Egyptian. Our blankets are originally pagan Turkish.

If we prefer eiderdowns - that's pagan Scandinavian. If we wear pyjamas - that's pagan East Indian. If they be silk - that's pagan Chinese. The spinning and weaving processes that put all these together for us are originally pagan Afghanistani. If we live their lives by timepieces - that has pagan origins too. The glass we drink water from is originally pagan Egyptian. The mirrors we look into (Mediterranean), the porcelain we use (Chinese), the glazed tiles we stand on (Babylonian) and the bath we take (Roman) are all pagan in origin. The idea of shaving is an ancient pagan Sumerian rite and if we use a razor - that's pagan Indian. Our towels are pagan Turkish, our chairs are pagan Palestinian.

Presumably we wear tailored clothes (first worn by pagan Mongols) and shoes - first worn by pagan Greek-Egyptians. If we eat food with a touch of sugar - that's pagan Indian. If they be pancakes (pagan African) with cream (pagan Greek) or eggs (pagan south-east Asian) on toast (pagan Scandinavian) with butter (pagan Egyptian) washed down with orange juice (pagan Mediterranean), we cannot avoid paganism. The coins we use to pay for these goods are originally pagan Mediterranean. And should they read this, they are reading points I am making using ancient pagan Semitic characters imprinted on an ancient pagan Chinese material we now call 'paper'.

In this light, Adventist critics of contemporary pop would do well to reassess what exactly it is about 'pagan' culture they object to - only the music? (7) Why not all of it? Or is that magnifying the law too much? Of course they have a right to throw what they define as 'pagan' Pop music out of their lives. But they should realise that there are also pagan babies in the bath-water of every culture - whether it be eighteenth century European or twentieth-century Hip-Hop.

II: The Fruit Argument

The authors reject the argument that this preference for European classical music with its concomitant emphasis on order, discipline and form is a cultural bias. The Winandys (writers) say they proved this by showing its accessibility to other ethnic groups. They report having been successful in turning Rwandans on to Bach. During their tenure at the Adventist University of Central Africa, they say he was the composer most preferred by Rwandan choir students under their tutelage. As they put it:

That's right! In the very heart of Africa you should have witnessed the choir's sensitivity when interpreting Jesu, Joy of Man's Desiring.

One can only add it is a pity the choir did not effect the same sensitivity in their Adventist audiences - many of whom took to carving each other up in recent genocidal conflicts which have stricken the country. More importantly, the unstated assumptions in the Winandy illustration and its experience are exactly that which fuels anti-mission cynicism and which sees it as an extension of European cultural imperialism. Colonialism and post-Colonialism can hardly be distinguished and represent a long and sad history which extends from the advent of Christianity to Coca-Cola, from Methodism to McDonald's. Adventists too have not always distinguished 'doing God's work' from 'doing cultural work'.

The *AA* contributors rail against 'rhythm' - that it is bad since it is overindulged in Rock and causes us to move our bodies in seductive patterns - is standard for most for the authors. And this is a pity. The point of all successful interactions is synchronisation whether we be talking, singing, marching, praying or picnicking. As social scientists have long observed, social intercourse works when eyelids and eventually heartbeats - our internal drummers - synchronise. (8) Music does this for us easily. It produces synchronisation quickly and effectively.

Yet this seems something to be feared among the *AA* authors. In this regard, they seem afraid of their bodies. Scared of what it might do if prejudice does not rule over it. Hence, they appear here to reflect the very pagan philosophical dualism they would eschew in relation to theological matters. They implicitly to hold an Apollonian (contra-Dionysian) view which seeks to repress free body language to formal mental structures. They implicitly view the body as something intrinsically evil and which has to be brought under the discipline of the mind. As one author puts it: *Satan's music at its worst is murky as a polluted stream and dissonant as sin. It bypasses the intellect in its appeal to the lower nature.*

There is no concession to the possibility that God (rather than the Devil) may speak through emotional passion and uninhibited physical fervour. (9)

AA authors also recite the alleged links between 'Rock' and promiscuity. Louis Torres for example, argues that 'Rock' leads to 'inherent sexual stimulation'. This is because 'Rock 'n' Roll' once referred to sex in the back seat of a car. I say 'once referred' because Rock is more generally thought of as a musical entertainment industry these days. For some reason, Torres thinks that what was once on the label necessarily still produces the effect. Even if this were true, and without conceding that for some Christians, sexual stimulation in the back seat of a car with one's partner may be just what is needed to spice up a flat marriage, Rock is nevertheless condemned out of hand as though this effect is guaranteed, as though it is universal, and as though only Rock Music can produce it.

Like Torres, the Winandys also make the sex and Rock equation. They think that since Elvis Presley equated Rock with sex, the rest of us have to. They certainly do. And since Rock necessarily equates with sex in their minds, they argue, 'Gospel Rock' must 'equal gospel (immoral) sex' [bracket theirs]. Just what immoral gospel sex amounts to (sex on the Sabbath?) is anyone's guess.

But as they put it: *amplifiers are employed to produce excessive noise [and]... when it is combined with the sexiness of rock and jazz rhythms, it has an almost irresistible effect on the sex organs.*

If this is true, then every amplified rock and gospel concert I have ever witnessed has been a massive failure. Certainly, hardly worth repeating. For despite what must be massive stimulation to the sex organs, people at these gatherings do not engage in uncontrolled sex acts. In fact quite the opposite - participants at Rock and Gospel concerts are *studious* in their sexual avoidance of each other. Sleaze is present - as it is in church for that matter - but it is certainly not the norm. Fun is - and it is not the same as having sex (despite what many think).

The Winandys go even further in their Rock-leads-to-sex argument: they say it has contributed to an 'increase in the numbers of teenage mothers'. That teenagers may simply have their radios or stereos tuned to rock while engaged in sex is not considered. To the Winandys this is not merely association but cause. They see no spurious relationship. An irrelevant variable is provocatively suggested as a causal one.

Admittedly the link between Rock culture and drugs is less contentious. And Richard Mendoza's autobiographical piece accurately reflects the reality for many musicians and their fans. But it is wrong to assume that what was once a personal problem is for all a necessary condition of Rock culture.

Many pop stars and lesser stars have eschewed drugs and continue to do so. (10) Moreover, despite an analysis of Muzak and its putative effect on us, it is fallacious to posit a view of humans as though we are Pavlovian stimulus-response subjects helpless in the face of musical-ideological conditioning. The messages we receive knowingly and unconsciously do not work on us in the way this hypodermic model of behaviour imagines. (11) Rather, we negotiate with what we encounter. We weigh up, we accept and we discard.

III: More Analytical Fallacies – in concept & method

These critics thereby commit themselves to an analysis (or lack of it) that presents difficulties for any reasonable thinker disturbed by fallacies which are either ecological, reductionist, tautological, teleological or spurious in nature.

For example, Jim Brackett tells us that 'there is music of heavenly origin' and that there is music which is not – 'the enemy has his music'. The trouble is that Jim presumes to tell us which is which. And so I ask which *is* which? Is the Heavy Metal Rock anthem structured on a Bach prelude 'heavenly' or 'one of Satan's substitutes' (as Brackett calls them)? Is a badly played and sung Christian hymn whose melody is based on a nineteenth century dance hall hit 'heavenly' or Satanic? What criteria do we have for knowing the difference?

What if we disagree on those criteria? Why should I defer to what Jim Brackett or any other person wants to insist on? Pete Geli Jnr simply tells the reader not to trust his/ her (pro-Rock) judgement but to simply go along with the (anti-Rock) arguments being put forward. This slavish submission to their authoritarianism is warranted because, as he says, we cannot trust our own judgements - they are too 'subjective'. Which again leaves the question begging - why should we trust theirs? Geli's answer is that he and his colleagues are (a) not issuing their own subjective judgements but (b) simply affirming the Biblical prescription. Whether (a) is true is arguable but even if it were, (b) is not consistent with their pronouncements. That is to say, what the Bible has to say about the matter of musical expression has clearly more in common with what they object to than what they affirm. (12)

Which brings us to yet another problem: the authors seem unable or unwilling to discriminate between the multiplicity of contemporary popular music forms - they simply lump them all under the rubric of 'Rock'(13). This allows them to make the breathtaking equation that 'Rock' (in all its variations) equals 'Satan'. The Winandys typically remind us that since Satan once conducted the heavenly choirs - choirs take note! - he must also be manipulating Rock music. I don't see the logical connection but it hardly matters to the *AA* contributors.

For them, the word 'Rock' is a cipher, a shibboleth which allows them and us to ignore hard thinking and substantive analysis of the matter. Like a label, a swearword, a stereotype which when applied to a person or social groups allows us to dismiss them without knowing them and what they are really like, 'Rock' has come to serve the same function for these *AA* writers. All 'Rock' is indiscriminately consigned to the garbage bin. Little attempt is made to distinguish a better popular song from a boring one, a constructive from a destructive one. No acknowledgment of the fact that culture is an arena of contestation, of ambiguity and of contradiction. (14) No recognition of the fact that Rock itself mirrors both the good and the bad in society, in people, and in nature. This is regrettable because an opportunity to make some useful cautions in regard to contemporary popular music goes begging. Again, this weakens their case. And Christians seeking a more intelligent critique will have to look elsewhere. (15)

On a more positive note, Lee Roy Holmes's contribution does offer a set of values useful for assessing the lyrical-ideological worth of contemporary Christian music. He suggests (a) doctrinal content, (b) literacy and intellectual quality, and (c) spirituality are all important. It is hard to disagree with this although the idea of just what is inductive of 'spirituality' leaves room for much diversity of opinion. Similarly, it is difficult to disagree with the Winandys when they assert that good music (as music) combines a balance of tune, harmony, rhythm and dynamics. But while they see European classical music as achieving elemental equilibrium in this regard, others may feel that there are many ethnic and contemporary popular music styles and forms which also accomplish this.

Other authors warn of the dangers music can play in rituals of apostasy. Paul Hamel illuminates the Holy Flesh fanaticism of Indiana Adventism - an episode about which Ellen White had something to say. Much is made of her testimony against 'bedlam' and 'noise' in worship but the authors are careful not to refer it necessarily to the worship styles of 'celebration' Adventists. However, the implied parallels between the Sinai Aaronic apostasy and the defections of celebration-style Adventist congregations from mainstream Adventism, particularly in the US, are hard to avoid.

Moreover, while we can applaud one author's judgement that 'our hymnal represents a really impressive selection of the best' of Christian hymnody, I am unclear as to what to make of the *AA* suggestion that congregational song leaders can make hymns 'more meaningful', 'enjoyable' and `interesting' by: *sometimes dividing the congregation so that males sing a portion of the hymn and females another portion.*

With all due respect, this is a practice most Adventists have been doing since childhood and if this is still an 'interesting' way of hymn singing, I can only imagine that watching paint dry must be positively orgasmic.

Of Men

With one exception, the contributors to the *AA* special issue are men, mostly middle-aged and mostly 'white' (in the American racial sense). Gender, age and race criteria wouldn't normally matter, but in this case they do. For while I have no doubt that the contributors are good and decent persons who passionately love their church and their faith, they make their case less worthy by omitting the perspectives of women, youth and African-American and non-American Adventists. But it is easy to see why - their critique as a whole is implicitly directed against these groups. (16)

Furthermore, a real problem with music criticism in Adventism is that for some reason, we are all experts. In the literary and artistic world at large, debate about the merit of Pop music is a field of intellectual-aesthetic inquiry generally marked by specialisation, years of training and credentials. Adventists, on the other hand, will just rush in like proverbial bulls in China shops holy horned and ready to gore anything or anyone that sounds 'worldly'. After which, having surveyed the wreckage created by often crude and irrational arguments against 'worldly' music, they seem stunned to find their young people have fled for greener, safer, saner, more relevant pastures.

While all of the contributors to this *AA* issue would feel qualified to speak on the topic of music - and as Adventists we have always valued a holy and forthright conscience - the question of whether they are as fully researched and informed on the topic as they could be, is another matter. Adventists are neither tomatoes nor mice and Rock is no more a Satanic plot than McDonald's.

Culture - popular or otherwise - is a field with many players possessed of many different motives. Cultural expression is neither apriori good nor bad, moral or immoral. The point is to test to see that which is good. To find that medium and expression which uplifts and to do it for God's glory. Whether it be classical, ethnic, world, new age, techno, or hip-hop is irrelevant.

In articulating its philosophy of music, Adventists would do well then to recognise the complexity and slippery ambiguities inherent in cultural analysis - of which Pop music and its criticism is but one expression. Neither will we achieve much by resolving present music debates by resiling to the gavel of 19thcentury authorities. Adventism needs to re-think its philosophy, acquire an artistic consciousness, and extend the spectrum of music it sponsors and promotes so that it reflects the range of music, which is actually out there in its pews. Its present policy is counter-productive to expressing the broadness and variegation of the musical gifts of the Holy Spirit. Administrators seem to want to pursue a narrow and 'safe' aesthetic which happily conforms to the reactionary values of an ageing elite (who happen to share class background and cultural tastes) but this ignores the needs and talents of a plural, regendered and multicultural membership.

Finally, in relation to the *AA* special issue, the critical condition of Western Christianity is such that a newer sophisticated analysis and praxis are called for. The new tele-technological consciousness springing from post-WWII cultural hybridities now define the global village and they threaten to deracinate hitherto authentic expressions of a Christian culture - expressions to which the AA authors typically romantically cling. But it is futile to repeatedly pontificate an agonistic moral panic about contemporary popular music and its alleged effect on Adventist Christians. The job, rather, is to put some Solomonic realism into the Adventist cultural perspective: to respond to the perversity of pop not with a thinly disguised ageist, sexist or ethno-racist agenda, not by ignoring culture and history, not with a confusion of ends with means, but with a rearticulation and resignification of what Philippians 4: 8 might mean in a post-modern world.

Footnotes:
(1) As evidenced by my teaching, since 1985, the subject, 'sociology of pop music'.

(2) As exemplified by my having written since 1969 some 120-plus contemporary gospel songs and by my continuing involvement in live and production work as a musician.

(3) Rock and the Church (Illinois: Creation House, 1971). Larson's earlier attack on Rock Music was *Rock and Roll: The Devil's Diversion* - a title indicative of the theme that conservative Americans have been running since the 1950s.

(4) Volume 12, No. 1 Spring 1998.

(5) Jim Brackett, Louis Torres, Lee Roy Holmies, Pierre Winandy, Richard Mendoza, Paul Hamel, Pete Geli jnr, Lawrence Maxwell, and the journal's late editor, C. Mervyn Maxwell.

(6) Lawrence Maxwell and Paul Hamel also take this line - see later discussion.

(7) Apologies to the American anthropologist, Ralph Linton who, in another context, first brought much of this to my attention. See R. Linton, The Cultural Background of Personality (New Jersey, Prentice-Hall, 1945); also his One Hundred per cent American in J. R. Landis, Sociology Concepts and Characteristics (U. S., Wadsworth, 1971).

(8) See for example, Randall Collins, *Theoretical Sociology* (US: Harcourt Brace Jovanovich, 1988) p. 201-203.

(9) See King David's naked dancing before the Lord, for example.

(10) I'm showing my age but artists as diverse as Cliff Richard, John Kay, John Fogerty and Frank Zappa for example, come to mind.

(11) In relation to pop music, see excellent discussions in Brian Longhurst, *Popular Music and Society* (UK: Polity, 1995); and Richard Middleton, *Studying Popular Music* (UK: Open University Press, 1990).

(12) See Psalms for example.

(13) Twentieth-century popular youth music includes: styles from folk-indigenous music such as Celtic, European, African, Arabic, Caribbean, South American, Indian, Asian; styles from `country' such as Western Swing, Honky-Tonk/Outlaw, Bluegrass; styles from Blues, such as Delta-Mississippi, Texas, Memphis, Chicago, New Orleans, West Coast, East Coast; styles from Jazz such as New Orleans-Dixie, Big-Band Swing, Tin Pan Alley, Bebop, Cool, Free-Avant-

Garde; and styles from Gospel which include Acapella soloists, Quartets, Southern Convention, Choral, White and Black. All of which have mixed and metamorphosed into hybrids such as Rhythm-n-Blues, Rockabilly, Rock-n-Roll, Pop, and Rock. Each of which possess in turn a range of styles such as Girl-Groups, Surf, Psychedelic, Soul, Southern Boogie, Heavy Metal, Progressive-Art, Fusion-Jazz, Funk, Punk, Latin, Disco, Reggae, and more recently Rap, Hip-Hop, House, Acid, World, Global Pop, Ethno, Techno, Tribal and Trance. Each of these musics, in turn, is typically differentiated by performers affecting more subtle styles and ideologies associated with ethnic, age, gender and geographical factors.

(14) See Berniece Martin, *A Sociology of Contemporary Cultural Change* (Oxford: Basil Blackwell, 1981).

(15) A useful starting place is Martha Bayles, *Hole In Our Soul* (New York: The Free Press, 1994). Bayles makes a worthwhile case for seeing bad pop music as that which is consistent with what she defines as 'perverse modernism' in popular culture. As a scholar and musician, Robert Walser, *Running With The Devil* (US: Wesleyan University Press, 1993) presents a sophisticated but positive case for Heavy Metal music.

(16) Various authors make little attempt to mask their cultural prejudices. From a sociological point of view, their ageism, racism, and to some extent sexism, are so palpable I can only imagine that 'they know not what they do'.

Appendix

Neale, Sally's album launch, poster, Wolfgramm Sisters, Jonah, Sally, Robert, SALT.

Seven Waves of Australian Rock

Robert Wolfgramm

> *Galilee was on the first wave of Jesus-Rock, but we were, in historical-cultural terms, part of what I think of as the 'seventh wave' of Australian Rock.*

The 80s should have been better, but they were pretty good nevertheless. Australian radio and TV were coming of age with good homemade rock finally, but it had been a long time incubating.

The first years of the 80s were also the last years of my brief recording career. The point I want to make here is that personally, as a 'Wolfgramm', I was a second- generation musician, a second waver. My piano-playing Dad (Robert), and his brother, Uncle Bill Wolfgramm were the first wavers of a family tradition. (My children, the Wolfgramm Sisters, are a third).

Uncle Bill was, as historian Nick Bollinger points out (in his *100 Essential New Zealand Albums*, 2009) the first New Zealand and indigenous Pacific artist 'to release an album'. He recorded 1956's *South Sea Rhythm* (my copy appears in Bollinger's book) which Bollinger rightly summarises 'as clean fresh and exciting today as when they were minted in the mid-50s'. He calls Uncle Bill's solos 'exquisite' and calls the album 'a perfect introduction to New Zealand's first homegrown guitar hero'.

In historical context, Galilee was on the first wave of Jesus-Rock, but we were, in historical-cultural terms, part of what I think of as the 'seventh wave' of Australian Rock.

1

First there were the 'Australian pioneers' who had been there at the beginning of recorded music with the first Australian pressings by Columbia Gramophone Company appearing in 1926.

The following year American hillbilly imports began arriving. By 1929 records by the 'Singing Brakeman' and Country music pioneer, Jimmie Rodgers, arrived on Australian shores. That year, Sydney-based Len Maurice *aka* Art Leonard was the first Australian to record on vinyl – doing cowboy song covers.

In 1930, records by American hillbilly royalty, the Carter Family, were being heard across Australia. Then in 1932, the first local popular music star appeared – the young Robert Lane, to become famous as Tex Morton, arrived from New Zealand. In 1936, Tex recorded originals (for the Columbia label) such as *Wrap Me Up In My Stockwhip & Blanket* and enjoyed a newfound popularity. Canadian hillbilly, Wilf Carter, was also popular at bush dances.

The first genuinely Australian star was Buddy Williams. In 1933, Buddy, an adoptee, ran away from his parents' farm on the New South Wales north coast. In 1939, influenced by the style and success of Tex Morton, Buddy recorded his own original compositions. One year later, his song *The Australian Bushman's Yodel* signalled the beginning of a specifically non-convict, 'Australiana' imagery in popular songs. Joining Buddy in this pantheon of pioneers was 16-yr old Queenslander, Shirley Thoms, who in 1941 became the first female soloist to record original songs.

The years of the Second World War also gave opportunities for other female artists such as 16-year old June Holmes and Dusty Rankin, to come into the public arena. In 1942 another Australian original, Smokey Dawson, recorded his own cowboy-style originals. But the end of the War brought two other names to the fore – names that changed forever what Australians would find acceptable. One was Gordon Parsons who in 1946 began his recording career. Along with poet, Dan Sheehan, Parsons co- authored the classic, *Pub With No Beer*

– a song made that ten years later became the first monster hit of Australian popular music by the second name, David Gordon Kirkpatrick, better known as Slim Dusty (RIP).

Slim's career began in 1947 with his recording of the song, *When The Rain Tumbles Down In July* – a classic co-written with his wife and manager, Joy McKean. This song became a favourite of mine. At this time Slim began his trademark touring, playing and singing his standards to audiences all over Australia – from country towns, to Aboriginal settlements to big cities. Slim perfected the 'bush ballad' formula along with Stan Coster and Shorty Ranger.

I don't know when I first heard Slim, but I first saw him live in the Victorian regional city of Geelong in 1977. I was truck driving interstate at the time and, winding my way home from South Australia one Friday or Saturday, I pulled up at a Geelong intersection where, hanging across the highway, was a banner advertising Slim's show that night in the Town Hall. I decided I would pull over and go have a look-see – more out of curiosity. What I found was the consummate family show. Unlike Rock concerts I had been to, Slim's audience comprised whole families – Mum, Dad, kiddies in their pyjamas, uncles, aunts, grandmas and grandpas were there. I was fascinated - little did I know that the following year I would meet the man himself with his wife Joy, and his daughter Anne Kirkpatrick – a Country rock star in her own right. And then, after performing in an outer Melbourne town, Croydon, one winter night in 1979, Slim's band came home to my place. I lit a fire while they drank and jammed the night away. It should have been recorded.

Along with Slim, the 1950s and 60s belonged to the unique Chad Morgan and Slim's brother-in-law Reg Lindsay who hosted a square-dance show on TV. Also in there was Aboriginal pop star, Jimmy Little (RIP), who had a monster hit with a song called *Royal Telephone*. He originated from Wallaga Lake – a sacred place in the dreaming of the Yuin people of the south coast on New South Wales.

In 1971 I had the privilege of meeting Jimmy in Newcastle NSW where a Maori singer called Ted Bennett was his support act. Ted wanted some orchestral backup and had the charts from his last recording session and he asked me if I could put an ensemble together and conduct it for him. I did and it was good, but Jimmy was definitely the headline act - the Newcastle Town Hall was packed with his adoring fans from all over.

As in America, these country-hillbilly singers were Australia's first wave of recording artists in popular music and they continued on through to the 80s and beyond. They began in country towns, fairs and big tents and ended up on prime-time TV.

2

Meanwhile, back in the late 50s, a second wave materialized as television was coming into its own. I arrived in Australia as that second wave from 1958- 63 was peaking. It included mostly individual artists, soloists, who mimicked the American Rock n Roll, R n B, Doo-Wop and early Surf artists.

They included what I've counted up as 'the five Johnnys' - Johnny O'Keefe, Johnny Devlin, Johnny Rebb, Johnny Ashcroft, and Johnny Chester, as well as Frank Ifield, Rolf Harris, and Col Joye. The leading female singers were Patsy Ann Noble, Lonnie Lee, Noeleen Batley and Betty McQuade.

3

A third wave of Australian rock began in the years 1963-1966 and, following the early Beatles and the Mersey beat, groups dominated.

They included Ray Columbus & the Invaders, Billy Thorpe & the Aztecs, the Seekers, Bobby (Bright) & Laurie (Allen), Bill & Boyd, the Easybeats, Ray Brown & the Whispers and MPD Limited. Individual artists were Little Pattie, Rob E.G. and Normie Rowe.

4

A fourth wave began in the years 1966-70 and these were groups influenced and modelled on the psychedelic group era.

They included the Loved Ones, the Twilights, the Masters Apprentices, the Cherokees, the Groove, Somebody's Image (featuring

Russell Morris), the Vibrants, the Bee Gees, the Groop, the Town Criers, the Valentines, the Flying Circus, Doug Parkinson In Focus, and Tamam Shud. Soloists were Ronnie Burns, Johnny Young, Johnny Farnham, Ross D Wylie.

5

A fifth wave of Australian rock formed from 1971- 1974. It was defined by more Country-Rock, Blues and R n B influences.

It included groups such as Daddy Cool, Mixtures, Spectrum, Chain, Blackfeather, Brian Cadd, La De Das, and Country Radio. Soloists and exceptions to this sound were the Moir Sisters, Ted Mulry, Kevin Johnson, Jamie Redfern, Helen Reddy, Allison Durbin, Olivia Newton- John, and Colleen Hewett.

6

The 70s saw a sixth wave in the years 1974-79 and these were artists affected by glam, disco, funk and heavy-metal, hard rock.

They included groups such as Sherbet, Skyhooks, Hush, Max Merritt & the Meteors, AC/DC, Little River Band, Air Supply, Ol' 55, The Sports, Dragon, Jeff St. John, and the Ferrets. Male soloists included Stevie Wright, William Shakespeare, John Paul Young, Richard Clapton, Mark Holden, Andy Gibb, Peter Allen, John St Peeters, and Jon English. Female soloists included Debbie Byrne, Sister Janet Mead, Linda George, Marcia Hines, and Renee Geyer.

7

The seventh wave formed in the years 1979-1983 and marked a transformation of Australian rock. It saw a maturation of song-writing and production techniques.

Characterising this new sophistication were groups like Split Enz, Mi-Sex, The Angels, Cold Chisel, Men At Work, Mondo Rock, Mental As Anything, Icehouse, INXS, Australian Crawl, Redgum, and Moving Pictures. Individualists who stood out were English-sounding Billy Field, Italian-sounding Joe Dolce, and Kiwi import, Sharon O'Neill.

At the back of the pack, were a handful of streetpreachers with their roots in several of the preceding waves of Aussie Rock and whose ranks included musos like Brian Patterson and Sam Melamed, and a bunch of fringe rockers and gospel-exponents like Galilee who could claim pedigrees of our own, as well as a borrowed heritage that was second to none – after all, SDA Pastor Richard Penniman was better known to the world as Little Richard, a co-founder of Rock n Roll and Rock itself.

The performance of Jonah. L-R: Lynda Bird, Genna Levitch, Lester Silver (standing), Simon Cowell and Paul Beaumont

Author Credits

Ivan Caldwell was the first musician to perform Robert's songs in public. Robert spent his early high school years living in the Caldwell household where both he and Ivan learned music from Ivan's father Dave. Ivan performed in Threedom, Jonah and Persecution Games and continues to sing Wolfgramm songs in his local church. He and his wife Debbie are available for performances: (02) 4329 2867 and deb54ivan@yahoo.com.au

Malachi Doyle is one of Robert's former Sociology students, from Monash University. A regular at the 'Café Bob's' (the Friday night jams held in the Wolfgramm home in the 90s), Malachi played a key role in Apocalypse Rider and subsequent Wolfgramm concerts. Often partnering with Terry McCarthy, Malachi currently has his own act, which has toured Europe & the US & performs in inner-Melbourne.
http://malachidoyle.bandcamp.com/
www.facebook.com/malachidoylemusic

Neale Farnell is a lead guitarist whose bands Drowning On Dry Land and Texas Flood also featured harmonica-player Colin Mack (featured on Refugee and Persecution Games). Neale performed and worked closely with Robert on Persecution Games and has continued to collaborate ever since. Texas Flood currently performs at Blues venues in and around Melbourne. Website:
www.melcharter.com/neale
www.facebook.com/TexasFloodTheBand
www.soundcloud.com/bill-ben or just Google him.

Sally Hilder is the featured vocalist on All My Friends Are Sinners and Persecution Games. After cutting these albums she ran her own Sally Hilder Band that performed in and around Sydney in the early-80s. She and husband Tom continue to perform in a band setup with varying musicians.

Anne Levitch was one of three wives supporting the Galilee boys when it was a concept being workshopped over a communal table. Her efforts included dividing up the bread and fish to feed the Galilee team when visiting, screen printing posters, and performing other sundry menial tasks as required. She continues to invest her professional time in creative industries.

Genna Levitch is the business manager of Galilee Records. In the late-70s he was the organizational brains behind the recording and distribution of All My Friends Are Sinners, Refugee and Persecution Games, also organising their re-release in 2013-2014. He played a role in the stage play Jonah and privately he has written poems for as long as anyone can remember.

Lester Silver wrote the musical Thomas, which shared a bill with Lowell's play Martin Luther at Ryde Civic Centre in 1973. They teamed up and created Jonah, in which Lester played the lead role. After this, Lester took up sitar and eventually travelled to India to further his understanding. Lester is now considered to be one of New Zealand's foremost sitar players.

Lowell Tarling co-wrote Threedom with Robert and has been a fulltime writer since 1980. His works include The Edges of Seventh-day Adventism, Tiptoe Through a Lifetime – the biography of Tiny Tim, and Taylor's Troubles, which is set at Strathfield SDA High School in 1962. Lowell is a Lyrics Judge for the Australian Songwriters Association (ASA).

www.lowelltarling.com.au

Stewart Walker was among the first to bring the guitar into church programs and social events. People forget how controversial it was in 1963 when he first did this. He continued performing for a decade in churches, at venues and even in the Domain. He played a leading role in Jonah.

Robert Wolfgramm is a Sociologist, a Bible translator (*NaiVolaTabu*, New Fijian Translation [NFT], songwriter, musician and record producer. He co-wrote Threedom, wrote/produced and performed on all three Galilee LP records, and also co-wrote a musical titled Apocalypse Rider (1998). He continues to write songs. In 2012 he was the recipient of the Gabe Reynaud Award at the Manifest Creative Arts Festival.

Glossary

Apocalyse Rider- a Christian musical, in the genre of Threedom, Thomas, redolent of Godspell, Jesus Christ Superstar and Joseph and the Technicolour Dreamcoat. Written by RW and LT, performed at Monash University, Frankston campus 1998, Avondale College 1999, and other Melbourne venues. Never recorded to CD.

ARTP – Adventist Radio & Television Production, Fox Valley Rd Wahroonga. Also a recording studio that released the SALT LP records, and now the venue for Psalter Music. It is currently known as the Adventist Media Centre.

Avondale College is the only tertiary educational institution operated by the SDA church in Australia. Situated at Cooranbong NSW, its location was chosen by EG White in 1898 as a result of a dream/vision she experienced on the site. It is a boarding college whose primary purpose is to train and prepare students for church employment. The three principals of Galilee attended the college from 1968-1973 with various levels of course completion. Co-located on Dora Creek with the church-owned Sanitarium Health Food company.

Commission the Sydney Seventh-day Adventist Church's most competent and popular band in the early 70s. Core members were: Jan Judd, Lyn Martin, Lyndria Maywald, Ivan Caldwell, Warren Judd, Dave McMahon, Graham Fletcher. Others in the lineup included Jenny Parr, Carl Needham, Archie Steele and Geoff Waters.

Desmond Ford, double PhD, popular and well known theologian, academic and Head of Theology Department at Avondale College in the late-60s. In 1980, Ford was defrocked by the SDA church, effectively terminating his employment in controversial circumstances. This event and the tumultuous times that followed gave impetus to many Galilee songs. Many disaffected believers left the church. Des Ford and his supporters formed *Good News Unlimited* to preach the gospel.

Fanfare was a 3-monthly combined gathering of Sydney SDA youth at the Ashfield Town Hall. It was the venue for most SDA musicians until superceded by SALT. The Saturday afternoon program featured 'Sabbath' music. And the Saturday evening program was the testing ground for electric guitars - and even drums. Most musicians and bands mentioned in this book performed Fanfare through various incarnations.

Food for Thought was a vegetarian restaurant in Chapel Street Prahan, developed by the Melbourne Streetpreachers as one of several of their outreach initiatives.

GATE (ie. Go And Tell Everyone) was the much smaller Newcastle NSW equivalent of SALT. It operated a Christian coffee shop where musicians included Brian Patterson, Smiley Martin, Ivan Caldwell, Archie Steel and many others.

Jonah had two performances as a high school play (1974) before being staged as a musical before audiences in Sydney, Newcastle, Maitland, Avondale and the Lyceum Theatre (1975). Music written by Lester Silver, the song *Father in Heaven* was written for Jonah.

Lilydale Adventist Academy – the only Adventist boarding school on the east coast of Australia, in Lilydale 35km east of Melbourne. Robert Wolfgramm boarded there in the late-60s.

Linda Lee Records was started by Kevin Broadhurst (known at the time as 'Brian Vogue'). Its first 45 rpm single was *How Great Thou Art* (Jan Judd), followed by the No 1 hit *Poison Ivy* (Billy Thorpe & the Aztecs). The record label was bought by Festival and the Linda Lee label's early recordings are an acknowledged part of the second wave of Aussie Rock.

Local Conference is the bottom organizational tier of the SDA church. The governing body, in Washington DC, is known as the General Conference. The world is then divided into 13 Divisions (Australia is in the South Pacific Division).Each Division is subdivided into Unions (Australia and NZ are in the Trans-Tasman Union), which are then divided into Local Conferences.

All churches in the Sydney basin are part of the Greater Sydney Conference. This structure enables the head of the world church to micro-manage every financial, doctrinal or institutional aspect of the organization. See *Edges of Adventism* by Lowell Tarling (amazon.com) for a detailed account of how doctrinal deviation arises and is dealt with by the church hierarchy.

Manifest is a three-day event sponsored jointly by Avondale College and Adventist Media. Its purpose is to honour and provide a forum for the creative members of the church. The program consists of workshops, debates, sharing, performances and conferring of awards in writing, visual art and music. It is held at Avondale College in March each year. Its ultimate accolade, 'for a Life Time of Creative Ministry' was awarded to Robert Wolfgramm in 2012.

Psalter Music is the recording arm of the Adventist Media Network. It produces, promotes and distributes Christian music performed by a variety of artists and has recently added a Heritage collection of 70s albums digitally remastered and re-released to CD.

The Renaldi Trio comprised Dave Caldwell (cello), Glen Nixon (violin) and John Truscott (piano), a well-loved group of church performers in the early-mid 60s. The trio regularly performed all over Sydney and further afield, in church services and in the evenings at church socials.

Quick Brothers Band was the second Seventh-day Adventist Rock band in the Sydney region, and the most significant because Harry Dustin was its drummer. Harry changed his name to Harry Young and along with his band The Sabbath charted with a hit single 'Wheat in the Fields'. Harry is still active in music, having recently replaced the late Billy Thorpe in Harry Young & the Aztecs.

SALT (ie. Share a Little Truth) was the brainchild of Pastor Bryan Craig. It was an umbrella name for a range of young people's activities, including street-preaching, youth gatherings, prayer telethons, musical productions and a magazine called Telos. It was a testament to Pr Craig's personal standing that he was able to achieve bold moves despite the conservative nature of the church administration.

Strathfield SDA High School is where the three Galilee principals met. Sally Hilder also attended this school. Established in the 1930s, it was the only secondary SDA school in the Sydney basin for years. It was sold in controversial circumstances in late 2012.

Streetpreachers (Sydney) – see SALT – originally began preaching in Manly but moved to the Sydney Domain, a public park that featured open air speakers on a range of political and religious subjects. They developed a format which included singing, backed by guitars, interspersed with short homilies.

Streetpreachers (Melbourne) were an autonomous outreach group arising from the Seventh-day Adventist Church, but outside church control and structure. For seven years they preached in Melbourne's CBD and won converts straight off the street. Their commitment to the Gospel message led to Insight worship sessions (at the McDougall residence), Melbourne's first vegetarian restaurant (Food for Thought) and support for Galilee Records. Names include: John, Peter & Jenny, Eric & Rhonda, Lianne& Vic, Con & Louise, Phil, Adrian, Colin, Harvey, Greg, Mark, Ag, Lucas, Julie, Jenni, Mark and the Wheatley Road mob.

Threedom was a folk cantata performed seven times 1971-1972 at Parramatta SDA Church, Hamilton SDA Church, Ryde Civic Centre and Avondale College. Never recorded, although in its day ARTP held preliminary discussions with Robert about releasing Threedom as a SALT LP record.

Wayfarers was the first Sydney-based Seventh-day Adventist band with drums. The band operated from the Hurstville Church in the early-to-mid-60s. The personnel were Allan Butler, John Furness, Clive Sandon, Terry Grace, Trevor Roy and Tony Roy.

The Yellow House was an artists' collective in Sydney, Australia founded by artist Martin Sharp. Between 1970-1973, the Yellow House in Macleay Street near Kings Cross, was a piece of living art and a Mecca to Pop Art. The canvas was the house itself and almost every wall, floor and ceiling became part of the gallery. Many well-known artists helped to create the multi-media performance art space that may have been Australia's first 24 hour-a-day 'happening'. Martin drew the b/w *Persecution Games* album cover for Galilee Records.

***

Review & Media Release

At first glance, *The Story of Galilee* might give the impression of a seditious group of teens who found voice for religious rebellion through music. This assessment understates the situation. It is impossible to ignore the authenticity of their collective and individual voices. Without doubt, their writing and performances arose from passion for their craft in both word and musical expression. However, viewing this experience without the wider perspective of a spiritual background and context fails to do justice to those represented in the pages of this book.

Whatever their current belief system or stated disclaimers for their present spiritual lives, this backdrop is as important as the rehearsing, crafting and staging for their performances. Although none of them would lay claim to anything beyond their collective collaboration, they not only spoke *to* a generation of Seventh-day Adventist youth, they spoke *for* them. And further still.

They arrived at a crisis time in the church. Cracks were beginning to appear in the very fabric of church organisation. It was with considerable vigour that church leaders attempted to quell the modern attitudes of youth and their questioning of doctrine.

Because a portion of this experience was accompanied by wayout clothing, long hair and Rock music – the powers-that-be felt the impact of any New Wave would be minimal and short lived. However, they had not allowed for the fact that a growing number of the 'miscreants' were intelligent, gifted and more importantly – in search of truth.

Disillusionment among the youth initially came from the gap between the religion they were taught and the spiritual life of Christ.

It is no coincidence that *Galilee* came into being at a time of Jesus people. This phenomenon was much more than a ripple influence – it was a collective awakening of conscience. It was also a reassessment of the core beliefs of Christianity, and more particularly, the rigid legalistic teachings of the Seventh-day Adventist church of the time.

As church leaders the world over found, to their loss, the movement was neither transient nor superficial. The gap not only widened but cracked open. The youth of the church were expendable, but the status quo was not.

While not connected to *Galilee*, Dr Desmond Ford, a leading SDA theologian, evangelist and college lecturer was perceived as having a parallel path. It is impossible to tell the story of Galilee without celebrating the role of Dr Ford, who proved a much greater threat to the SDA equilibrium than a group of singers and performers. In a very clear sense, he put 'theos' back into theology with his gospel based 'Jesus Only' teaching. Dr Ford had no agenda to upset the balance of the church, or church leaders. However, a chasm resulted that sent shock waves through every level of the organisation.

Galilee was born of the desire to focus on Jesus of Galilee. The god/man who broke the rules, mixed with every level of society, failed to conform to ceremony and offered full and free pardon to all. The god to whom no one was expendable. The god who desired to be 'up close and personal' with humanity. The god who was broken, tested and tried. *Galilee* was drawn to the real Jesus, the man of sorrows, of the wilderness, of dark days and nights. The Jesus who trembled at the thought of the path ahead, and who said, 'Father, why have you forsaken me?' at his last earthly hurdle.

This was the Jesus of the people. A Jesus to be desired and sought, a Jesus to sing about.

Galilee was inconvenient. A phrase snatched from one of Dr Ford's sermons has unique relevance, 'God came to comfort the afflicted, and afflict the comfortable'.

Manifest has set out to achieve what earlier generations set aside – healing the breach. The first step towards recognition of the contribution of *Galilee* came with the honouring of Dr Robert Wolfgramm. It is the hope of many that this is a new beginning.

It is with great pleasure that I celebrate, not only the book *Galilee*, but also the rebirth of *Galilee Records* – to past generations who began a new wave of Christian music, but also to a new generation of truth seekers, heart teachers, gospel preachers and music lovers.

The *Galilee* recordings, CD's, lyrics, archives and more are available through www.galileerecords.com.au.

Linda Ruth Brooks

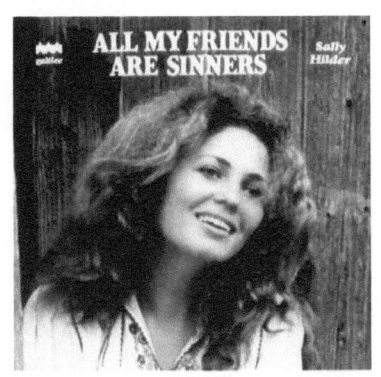

www.galileerecords.com.au
for CD's, lyrics, archives and more

www.ingramcontent.com/pod-product-compliance
Lightning Source LLC
Chambersburg PA
CBHW031416290426
44110CB00011B/405